HALI KEELER WITH LESLIE EVANS AND DAVID ROSE

Published by Haunted America
A Division of The History Press
Charleston, SC
www.historypress.net

Front cover: The entry gates at Fort Griswold. *Courtesy of Gerry Keeler.*

First published 2016

ISBN 978-1-5316-9942-0

Library of Congress Control Number: 2016934654

Of all the properties in Groton Bank that are of historical importance, the Amos Prentice House on Thames Street, also known as the Mother Bailey House in honor of its most colorful and famous occupant, is in the most extreme state of disrepair. Having been in private hands for decades, it has been virtually ruined by thoughtless renovations and careless tenants. It was bought by the City of Groton to save it from further deterioration and remains empty. The house, including the famous tavern in the basement, needs complete restoration, from a purely structural perspective to an eventual esthetic one.

Some of us in the community thought that if we could just paint the downstairs rooms, hang some period artwork and furnish it lightly with some historically accurate pieces, it could be open to the public on a limited basis for tours, which would create some revenue. However, the structural engineers have deemed the building too unsafe even for that. The ghost tours have raised a few hundred dollars, but that is a drop in the bucket.

Therefore, we dedicate any royalties from the sale of this book to the future restoration of this important house and look forward to the day when it can take its rightful place among the active historic house museums in southeastern Connecticut.

CONTENTS

PREFACE

Groton is an area of about seven square miles bordered on the east by the Mystic River, the west by the Thames River and the south by Fisher's Island Sound. Its history has been chronicled in detail by Carol Kimball, the late town historian of Groton. The depth of her knowledge and the breadth of her collection have provided extensive resources. When she passed away in 2010 at the age of ninety-four, her estate contained boxes and files of research, clippings, notes, books and artifacts that have not yet been entirely catalogued. It is a treasure-trove of historical information, much of which was given by the family to the Groton Historic Society. Jim Streeter, the current town historian, also has a collection of boxes and closets and rooms filled with his own research. Between the two of them, there is very little that is not known about the history of Groton. I am relying on the fruits of their combined efforts to create this preface.

Groton's beginnings can be traced to 1646, when John Winthrop Jr., son of the governor of Massachusetts, settled on the Thames River and established what he called the Pequot Plantation. According to *The Groton Story*, by Carol Kimball, in June 1646, it was recorded in Governor Winthrop's journal that "a plantation was begun this year at Pequod river by Mr. John Winthrop, Jr., Mr. Thomas Peter, minister, and this court power was given to them two for ordering and governing the plantation until further order, etc."

This settlement extended to both sides of the river, but the east side was originally used for grazing cattle. In 1647, John Winthrop Jr.'s family came from England to live in a large house in Pequot Plantation. He also was granted land on the east side of the river; this was considered the best farmland in town. Later that year, other plots of land where given by lottery, and families were attracted to the good land of Poquonnock Plains, a fair distance from the river on the east side. One of these plots was described as "a parcel of land between the west side of the Mystic River and a high mountain of rocks." Another was described as "where the wigwams were in the path that goes from his house toward Culvers among the rocky hills." (Edward Culver had a farm nearby). If it sounds like there were a lot of rocks, ask anyone who has tried to put in a lawn or garden in this area. Rocks seem to spontaneously generate around here. To be fair, though, we have an abundance of beautiful old stone walls, which did—and continue to—make good fences.

In 1657, after eleven years of petitioning, John Winthrop Jr., recently elected the third governor of Connecticut, quickly convinced the General Court that Pequot Plantation should be renamed New London.

Meanwhile, the problem was that although everyone was required to attend church services on the Sabbath, the only church in New London was on the west side of the river. This presented a problem for the families on the east side of the settlement, as roads were not very good, and even in poor weather they were forced to cross the river on the ferry. A ferry, at that time, was basically a scow-type, flat-bottomed boat that operators poled, rowed or sailed across the water. It was both dangerous and uncomfortable, but it was the only way to cross a river in the 1600s. Around 1687, James Avery, who was settled on the east side of the river, pleaded for separation from New London, as at that time twenty-eight families were living there. He asked that they be allowed to have their own church, which was at the heart of the problem. After nine years, they were allowed to have the minister come to the east side for church services—only once every third Sunday in inclement weather! Finally, in 1696, they were permitted to organize their own church, and in 1703, their meetinghouse was built. In 1705, the General Assembly approved and granted a charter to the lands on the east side of the Thames River. They were given full independence from New London. It is commonly believed that they called their new town Groton, after the Winthrop estate in England. (However, not everyone was pleased with that; some preferred the names Southwork or East London.) Whatever they called it, New London had the last word by demanding payment for the financial loss this would cause and ownership of the ferry.

Back to the church: the first one was Congregational, the established church of colonial New England. By 1704, some families were petitioning for a Baptist church, and consequently, Groton became home to several more Baptist, as well as Methodist, Episcopal and Lutheran, churches.

Once again, according to Kimball's *The Groton Story*, no sooner had the ink dried on the charter than a town meeting was called in 1706 to create a school. By 1766, all Connecticut towns were divided into school districts in order to receive a portion of public funds. There were numerous one-room neighborhood schools that children would attend. In 1864, school was in session in the summer and winter. By 1872, there were eleven districts: Groton Bank, North Lane, Center Groton, Burnett's, Mystic River, Upper Noank, Pequonnoc, Shinnicossett, Flanders, West Mystic and Noank. By 1929, there were twelve schools. There was no high school. By 1963, there were sixteen elementary schools, three junior high schools and one senior high. Sadly, today, there are only seven elementary schools, two middle schools and one high school.

According to an account in a Groton Patrolmen's Benevolent Association booklet from around 1958, from Jim Streeter's collection of historical files, quoting an earlier document, "The township is uneven, being hilly and abounding in rocks. A narrow tract extending along the Sound, and another extending up the Thames to a considerable distance from its mouth, are pleasant and fertile, but the remainder is difficult of cultivation…There are five villages in the township, each of which is a post office—Groton Centre in the north, Mystic River in the east, Noank and Poquonnock in the south, and Groton Bank in the west." To this day, these are still distinct geographic areas, fire districts or political subdivisions in Groton.

Speaking of which, in 1900 a petition was submitted to the General Assembly seeking to incorporate the "Bank" and the eastern shore of the Thames River as a "borough" of the town of Groton. The legislature approved it in 1903, and the borough of Groton was incorporated as a new political subdivision of the town of Groton. The borough was originally governed by a warden and burgesses system, still used by many towns today. In 1964, the borough became the city of Groton, which uses a mayor and council system of government.

The location on the Thames River attracted several large industries, including the Electric Boat Division of General Dynamics, Pfizer Pharmaceuticals and the Coast Guard Training Station (now Coast Guard Research and Development). These companies brought thousands of families to the area. All three of these industries are still here, although they have gone through periods of downsizing, expansion and back again. Electric Boat—or EB, as it is commonly known—builds submarines that eventually make their way to the U.S. submarine base farther up the river. The river is an integral part of these concerns.

Thames Street—originally called Bank Road, as it runs along the east side of the Thames River—was the main business district for Groton. It was a narrow dirt street and people traveled by horse, horse and carriage or oxen and carriage to carry out their tasks. An occasional stagecoach would pass through as well, often on its way to the ferry. Business was booming on Thames Street by 1910, and tracks were laid to accommodate the new trolley. Trolleys and horses were common sights every day. Once cars came along in the 1920s and '30s, the appearance of horses and oxen diminished.

Interestingly, when Thames Street was reconstructed beginning in 2013, parts of the trolley tracks were exposed and eventually dug up in pieces. Several lucky residents in the city were able to scavenge a little piece of history

By the late 1950s, there were seventy businesses on Thames Street. Today, there are fewer than twenty-five. But in its heyday, there was nothing like Thames Street for the local shopper.

Janet Downs, a Groton native, born and raised in the borough and a contributor to this book, has wonderful memories of growing up on Groton Bank. Her narrative follows.

Groton: A Childhood Tour

When I was growing up in the 1950s and early 1960s, Thames Street was the commercial and retail center of Groton. Grocery shopping necessitated a trip "downstreet," either on foot or by bus to either A&P or Beit Brothers. The mode of transportation would be determined by the amount of groceries to be purchased. The two stores, hardly "supermarkets" by today's standards, were located in two of Thames Street's brick buildings. Until a few years ago, one of these buildings housed the Thames Army Surplus store; the other building, at the foot of School Street, was destroyed by fire and exists today as a sad and truncated shell.

Other stores on the street included Youth Colony, a children's clothing store, and Krieger's Drug Store, which I remember as including a soda fountain with red vinyl stools. Edgecomb & Poppe, an old-fashioned "dry goods store," occupied the building that has now housed Paul's Pasta for more than twenty-five years. The area in the front window is now the location of the pasta machine; then it was the site of a wooden rack that held penny candy—Mary Janes,

Sugar Daddies, jawbreakers, colored candy dots stuck on long rolls of white paper and miniature wax soda bottles containing variously colored syrups.

It should be noted that while it was customary to go "downstreet" for everyday items, one was expected to go "overtown" to New London to shop for anything out of the ordinary, such as an outfit for a special occasion.

A significant number of doctors and dentists maintained offices along Thames Street. Among them were my family physician, Dr. Berwyn Force, and my dentist, Dr. Martin Feldman, both of whose offices were located in the building at the corner of Thames and Latham Streets. Whenever I had an appointment after school, I simply walked down the steep hill from Groton Heights School to the doctor or the dentist.

A gray ramshackle building on the river was the home of Gott's Garage. My father had taken his cars to Gott [Gottlieb Guhring] for many years, and when it was time to buy a car for me, it was Gott who persuaded him to buy the sensible blue sedan instead of the red convertible that I really wanted. My dad was right to take Gott's advice; the sensible used 1961 Falcon was driven by three generations of my family through the late 1970s.

As the town's main thoroughfare, Thames Street was often the venue for parades and special events. The annual Yale-Harvard Regatta held on the Thames River drew hundreds of spectators as well as vendors to line the sidewalks. The "Miss Rheingold" contest brought beautiful young women who waved to the crowds from open cars as they cruised slowly down the street. Later, both adults and children were given the opportunity to vote on who should be crowned "Miss Rheingold."

Farther south, at the five corners, stood the Groton Movie Theater where local children were introduced to Bambi, Snow White, Cinderella and the other Disney characters that sparked the imaginations of our generation.

The 1950s version of the convenience store was represented by a tiny shop on Monument Street and a slightly larger one at Thames and Broad Streets called the "Little Big Store." At both locations, penny candy, soda and comic books were in abundance.

The building of Groton's two shopping centers, the Groton Shopping Plaza and the Groton Shoppers' Mart, in the late 1950s sounded the death knell for Thames Street as a retail and commercial hub. One by one, businesses closed or relocated until at the present time, only a handful of businesses remain, including the tiny Borough Station Post Office and the venerable Ken's Tackle Shop.

Nevertheless, several institutions that played significant roles in the lives of many Groton children are still very much alive and well in Groton

Bank. I attended Sunday school and sang in the cotta choir at the Groton Congregational Church, an imposing stone building at the corner of Monument and Meridian Streets. Meetings of my Brownie and Girl Scout troops were held in its basement, as were potluck suppers and church bazaars.

The lovely Richardsonian Romanesque Bill Memorial Library, also on Monument Street, with its collection of birds, butterflies and the mysterious mummy's hand, was a place of wonder for me. The two librarians, Mrs. Chester and Mrs. Marquardt, could not have been more different in appearance. Mrs. Chester was tall, thin and angular with dark hair drawn back in a bun; I can see her wearing a green dress with a white lace collar. Mrs. Marquardt, on the other hand, was short, round and soft, with gray hair that framed her face and a preference for floral prints. Both were unfailingly kind, even as they maintained the library's quiet and decorum.

Unfortunately, Groton Heights School, a stately brick Beaux-Arts building with panoramic views of the Thames River, was closed a decade ago due to functional obsolescence. The sight of the abandoned school building is a source of sadness to me, as it must be to many others who spent their early years within its walls.

Next door, however, Fort Griswold Battlefield State Park, the site of a major battle of the Revolutionary War, remains unchanged from my childhood, as does the Groton Monument, a 135-foot-tall granite obelisk built in 1830 to commemorate the battle. Playing in the fort on summer afternoons and racing to the top of the monument will always be among my fondest memories of childhood.

Summer recreation in Groton was centered on Eastern Point Beach. I rode to swimming lessons in my neighbor's station wagon, along with their eight children. The Fourth of July was celebrated with fireworks in Washington Park. In winter, there was ice skating on the pond and sledding on Park Avenue. The pond is no longer flooded for skating, and Park Avenue was closed off in the 1970s. But families still come with their sleds to enjoy winter days in the park.

Groton is like all towns in that while much has changed, much has remained the same. It is still a good place to live, and many of us who grew up here have chosen to remain. Groton is a place where we value the past while looking forward to the future.

ACKNOWLEDGEMENTS

There are so many people whose help made this book possible. I'd like to thank, of course, Leslie Evans, director of the Avery-Copp House Museum, and David and Shirleyann Rose, current and former president of the Friends of Fort Griswold, for their chapters. Their knowledge and expertise could not have been replicated. Thanks go to Mayor Marian Galbraith for her extensive knowledge of the Mother Bailey House and her many notes and photos. Jim Streeter, Groton town historian, has amassed an enormous collection of vintage postcards of our area that he graciously donated to Avery-Copp Archives—they are a remarkable resource. Thanks also go to Jim for contributing his resources to the creation of the preface.

Gratitude goes to Janet Downs and Gerry Keeler for their photography skills and overall support and again to Janet for sharing her stories of growing up in the "'hood" that she contributed to the preface. Thanks also go to Joanie DiMartino for sharing her very interesting experiences at the Avery-Copp House.

Hats off, as well, to all of the business owners and residents who so generously shared their stories.

Many thanks to Shamus Denniston and the Thames Society of Paranormal Investigations (TSPI) for the "lockdowns" they carried out for some of our sites, providing us with amazing evidence, audio recordings and spectral images. The documentation of their investigations is flawless and the experience was amazing.

Finally, our appreciation goes to the souls who made this book possible.

INTRODUCTION

To say that there are a number of historic sites and associations in Groton, Connecticut, would be an understatement. Home to the Fort Griswold Battlefield State Park, the site of the only major Revolutionary War battle fought on Connecticut soil, it was also home to a prosperous maritime culture of shipbuilding and whaling. Homes of sea captains dot this neighborhood, known as Groton Bank for its location on the Thames River. Rich in history and folks who love it, it is a breeding ground for historic activities.

Many of the same people share these interests and are actively involved with each of these places, including Friends of Fort Griswold, the Avery Association, the Avery-Copp House Museum, the Bill Memorial Library and so on. It was no surprise that the topic of ghosts often came up. After all, with this much history, much of it deadly, how could there not be ghosts?

I am mostly oblivious to what might be happening in the realm of the supernatural, but I have lived in houses where unexplained events occurred. In the house in which I grew up, in urban South Norwalk, Connecticut, there was a third floor with a guestroom, an office and a small playroom. This was where my friends and I would gather as teens to play with the Ouija board. Over onion dip and chips, we had great fun asking it questions that were, for the most part, frivolous. There were a couple of occasions, however, when a corner of that room would grow cold, and we could hear footsteps on the stairs. One night, a friend and I slept in the guest room; as I got up to get a drink of water in the middle of the night, I turned to the bedroom door and saw what I thought was my friend standing there—a tall girl in a long nightgown. As I began to speak to her, she disappeared. This was the first sighting of our very own "woman in white." She was spotted on other occasions by those who slept in that room, always in the doorway. Footsteps on the stairs were a regular occurrence reported by guests who slept there, and footsteps along the second floor could be heard from the first—of course when no one else was at home. Even my father, who tended to brush these things off, came home one night to a completely empty and dark house, with the exception of a light burning on the third floor. He did admit to the hairs on his neck standing up when he went up to turn the light off.

Another house I lived in after I was married was in a clearing in the middle of the woods. Shortly after moving in, I returned home from work one day to find that the contents of the top shelf of one kitchen cabinet were neatly arranged in a row on the counter. Doors were locked; no one was at home. Since then, lights have gone on and alarms have gone off in the middle of the night; on one such occasion, the sense of someone sitting down on the bed got me out in a hurry! My daughter and I have both heard voices on occasion as well. I couldn't explain any of it. There is, at least for me, a big difference between experiencing unexplained events and being "sensitive" to the paranormal.

I do have a healthy respect for those who are. If someone like me could have these experiences, who knows what others might have? We shared the stories we knew and were interested enough to bring in a paranormal investigation group to see what else we could find. From this grew the Ghosts of Groton Bank walking tours, which began in 2012. Conducted at twilight in October, capitalizing on Halloween, the tour includes properties that were known or suspected to be haunted. The tours have been very successful—they mostly sell out—and the modest fees that are collected are donated in support of the restoration of the Mother Bailey House, one of the most significant but poorly maintained sites in the neighborhood. It spent years in private hands, broken up into apartments, and is in sad shape; its subsequent sale to the city has kept it from deteriorating. It is also the most popular site on the tour both for the stories and the docent who tells them.

It was at a chance visit to The History Press booth at the New England Independent Booksellers Association (NEIBA) trade show that introduced me to the Haunted America series. (As a librarian, I am attracted to trade shows like ants to honey!) I had the chance to read a couple of their books and thought that our story could make a good book, too! I was encouraged to contact them, and here we are. My collaborators on the book—Leslie Evans of the Avery-Copp House Museum; David and Shirleyann Rose of the Friends of Fort Griswold; and Janet Downs, lifelong neighborhood resident and a trustee of the Avery-Copp—came together on this project. Their combined knowledge, interest and great ghost stories served us well.

Once word got out about this project, ghost stories started coming to us. Casual asides—such as "did you know that the house I lived in was haunted?" "Have you spoken to so-and-so about what goes on in his place?"—came from all over. On one of the ghost tours, I was taken aside by a gentleman as he told me about his house. A casual remark at a party brought me another story of spooky goings on.

Putting this book together has been a lot of fun for us. We wanted to emphasize the rich and amazing history of our area, as well as entertain you with our experiences. We hope you enjoy them.

HALI KEELER

1

Fort Griswold: Still on Watch?

By David Rose

A Little History

Crossing the Gold Star Bridge on I-95 north, the traveler gets his first view of the city of Groton, nestled on the east bank of the Thames River. It looks at first like a quaint New England village, and while that is its heritage, the city is much more. The city is steeped in history. Originally, Groton was part of New London, but after establishing a church on the east side of the river in 1705, the residents were allowed to separate and form their own town. The borough of Groton, a subdivision of the town of Groton, was established in 1905, and in 1964, the borough was incorporated as the city of Groton.

In the colonial period, most of the population was settled along the bank of the Thames River, and the land was primarily used for farming and lumbering. Small businesses and shops were established to meet the needs of the people of Groton. Carol Kimball tells us about the colonial population in the following sections, taken from her book *The Groton Story*.

Groton's Maritime Heritage

With waterways at hand and good farmland scarce, Groton residents were destined for seafaring. Every man knew how to use an axe and building tools and with a little supervision could become a shipwright. Often he would combine this trade with farming and woodcutting for a livelihood. Most of the community was involved in building vessels, sailing them or furnishing cargoes for them to carry.

The first traders sailed to Boston and Plymouth to barter peas, Indian corn, cheese, pork or beef for tools, gunpowder or clothing. Boston vessels first provided prosaic necessities but later carried all kinds of "English goods" to make life easier. The earliest Groton shipbuilder whose name we know was John Leeds, a sea captain from Kent, England. By marrying Cary Latham's daughter Elizabeth he got the use of the convenient shipyard by the ferry. His 20-ton brigantine TRYALL sold for 80 pounds in 1683. Thomas Starr had a Groton yard opposite Winthrop's Neck where he built sloop SEA FLOWER, "a Square-sterned vessel of 67 tonns" in 1710. William and Thomas Latham built vessels farther south on Groton bank where the General Dynamics plant is located now. Thomas once launched a 100-ton brig with mast standing, fully rigged.

In 1723 came Groton's first experience with building big ships. Two Englishmen, James Sterling and John Jeffery, petitioned for a 12-year lease on the shipyard by the town ferry. A town meeting granted the request "provided that the persons build the great ship." Sterling and Jeffery produced a 700-ton vessel, the largest merchantman built in America before the revolution. Her construction attracted many skilled workers, causing the first of such immigrant waves so characteristic of the town's history. One brisk October day in 1725 a great concourse of people gathered at the ferry landing to watch the launching of the great ship. Joshua Hempstead reported that she went off "as upright as possible." She sailed for Lisbon the following August.

Jeffery also launched other vessels including a "pink-sterned ship" and a scow in which Capt. John Ledyard made a profitable voyage to England in 1738, enabling him to build a large warehouse next to the ferry.

Sturdy smaller vessels built on Groton's shore clung to their profitable trade with Caribbean Islands. Barbados was the favorite, but they also traded with Antigua, Jamaica, Tortuga and Guadalupe, ignoring the considerable hazards. In 1738 John Walsworth of Groton lost his sloop in a hurricane. Capt. John Ledyard weathered a bad storm but lost his cargo of 17 horses and 40 sheep. In Guadalupe smallpox claimed the life of Capt. Youngs Ledyard in 1762, "A gentleman endowed with many valuable Accomplishments."

Profits were worth the risks. Farm produce, salt fish, barrel staves or ice could be sold in the West Indies for cash or traded for a cargo of sugar, cotton, rum or molasses. Horses were in great demand. So many were shipped that sea captains of the day were jokingly called horse jockeys. Groton's Capt. William Latham exchanged one of Joshua Hempstead's horses for a hogshead of rum and a barrel of molasses.

If Groton townsfolk needed cloth, scythes, nails, glass, pewter, firearms, cutlery or brass, these manufactured items had to come from England. The New London Summary advertised in 1763:

Lately imported from London and to be sold by Dudley Woodbridge at his store in Groton, a small but neat assortment of English goods at the lowest rates.

MILITARY HISTORY

Though still an English colony, our settlers' toehold on the North American coast lay thousands of miles from England's armed might and they had to be ready to defend themselves. Every man between 16 and 60 belonged to a militia company or "'trainband,'" which drilled on periodic training days, always on the New London side until 1692, when Groton's first military company was formed.

The militia was ready in 1675 for New England's last struggle with the Indians when King Philip attacked settlements in Massachusetts and Rhode Island in the vain hope of driving the English from the land. In this conflict Groton's James Avery commanded 40 soldiers plus a band of Indians and under Capt. George Denison of Stonington carried on a successful mopping-up operation to quench the last sparks of Indian resistance. Family records credit Avery with the capture of 239 enemy Indians.

After Philip's defeat Indians never again threatened New England, yet there was no peace. Our colonists were involved in endless conflicts between the English and European powers, especially Spain and France. Groton's exposed coastal position prompted the town to provide ammunition for public protection in1731 and to distribute powder, lead and flints to the three militia captains, Ebenezer Avery, Christopher Avery and Daniel Eldridge.

In 1739 Groton was alerted for war with Spain; in 1743 they were called to help with a war with France. Six years later they were entangled in the French and Indian War. When that conflict ended at last in 1760 nearly

20 percent of the men in Connecticut had served in the campaigns, an experience most useful in the coming struggle for independence![1]

Groton was later the site of the Battle of Groton Heights, the bloodiest battle, based on population, of the American Revolution. Later, Groton was known for shipbuilding and whaling and, after the Industrial Revolution, became involved in manufacturing. During World War II, General Dynamics' Electric Boat Division was turning out submarines to help the American Naval Forces defeat the Axis powers. After the war, Pfizer Inc., a New York–based chemicals manufacturer, established its largest chemical and pharmaceutical manufacturing and research facilities in Groton.

THE FORT

Part of Groton's mystique is the number of ghost sightings and stories that have materialized over the years. Are ghosts roaming the earthworks of Fort Griswold?

Construction on Fort Griswold was started in 1775 on a hill overlooking the harbor of the Thames River. By 1781, the fort was completed and was a very impressive fortification. Construction was taking place in New London on Fort Trumbull, situated on a rise above the river, but it was not completed on the day of the battle. These fortifications were not fully staffed due to a lack of funding to pay the soldiers. After years of war, Connecticut, like most of the other colonies, was having financial difficulties. Most of the garrison stationed at Fort Griswold was furloughed, with some having been sent to other detachments. All that was left at the fort was a squad of sentries.

On Thursday, September 6, 1781, the people of New London and Groton, Connecticut, arose to a quiet, normal day as they started their usual chores. The day would change drastically, however, for those two towns, and it would take years for them to recover.

Around dawn, sails were spotted at the mouth of the river. These ships were thought to be a raiding party, and the alarm of two cannon shots was fired to alert the communities. A Connecticut native, Benedict Arnold, was in charge of the enemy forces. He was aware of what the cannon fire meant and immediately ordered that a third shot be fired from one of the ships. The three cannons shots signified that a local privateer was returning home. Much confusion ensued. Some residents continued with their chores while others armed themselves with muskets and raced to the forts to see for themselves what was happening. We are fortunate to have a firsthand account of the battle and its aftermath from Stephen Hempstead.

Stephen Hempstead's Account

The enemy landed in two divisions, of about 800 each, commanded by that infamous traitor to his country, Benedict Arnold, who headed the division that landed on the New London side, near Brown's farms; the other division, commanded by Colonel Ayres, landed on Groton Point, nearly opposite. I was first sergeant of Captain Adam Shapley's company of state troops, and was stationed with him at the time, with about twenty-three men at Fort Trumbull, on the New London side. This was a mere breast-work or water battery, open from behind, and the enemy coming at us from that quarter, we spiked our cannon, and commenced a retreat across the river to Fort Griswold in three boats. The enemy was so near that they overshot us with their muskets, and succeeded in capturing one boat with six men commanded by Josiah Smith, a private. They afterwards proceeded to New London and burnt the town. We were received by the garrison with enthusiasm, being considered experienced artillerists, whom they much needed, and we were immediately assigned to our stations. The fort was an oblong square, with bastions at opposite angles, its longest side fronting the river in a northwest and southeast direction. Its walls were of stone and were ten to twelve feet high on the lower side, and surrounded by a ditch. On the wall were pickets, projecting over twelve feet; above this was a parapet with embrasures, and within a platform for the cannon, and a step to mount upon to shoot over the parapet with small arms. In the south west bastion was a flag-staff, and in the near side, near the opposite angle, was the gate, in front of which, was a triangular breast-work to protect the gate, and to the right was a redoubt, with a three pounder in it, which was about 120 yards from the gate. Between the fort and the river was another battery, with a covered way, but which could not be used in this attack, as the enemy appeared in a different quarter. The garrison, with the volunteers, consisted of about 160 men. Soon after our arrival the enemy appeared in force in some woods about half a mile southeast of the fort, from whence they sent a flag of truce, which was met by Captain Shapley, demanding an unconditional surrender, threatening at the same time to storm the fort instantly if the terms were not accepted. A council of war was held, and it was the unanimous voice, that the garrison was unable to defend themselves against so superior a force. But a militia colonel who was then in the fort, and had a body of men in the immediate vicinity, said he would reinforce them with 2 or 300 men in fifteen minutes, if they would hold the fort. Colonel Ledyard agreed to send back defiance, upon the most solemn assurance of immediate succor. For this purpose Colonel —— started, his men being then in sight; but he was no more seen, nor did he even attempt a diversion in our favor. When the answer to their demand had been returned by Captain Shapely, the enemy was soon in motion, and marched with great rapidity, in a solid column, to within a short distance to the fort, where, dividing the column, they rushed furiously and simultaneously to the assault of the southwest bastion and the opposite sides. They were, however, repulsed with great slaughter, their commander mortally wounded, and Major Montgomery, next in rank, killed, having been thrust through the body, whilst in the act of scaling the walls at the southwest bastion, by Captain Shapely. The command then devolved on Colonel Beckwith, a refugee from New Jersey, who commanded a corps of that description. The enemy rallied and returned the attack with great vigor, but were received and repulsed with equal firmness. During the attack a shot cut the halyards of the flag, and it fell to the ground, but was instantly remounted on a pike-pole. This accident proved fatal to us, as the enemy supposed it had been struck by its defenders, rallied again, and rushing with redoubled impetuosity, carried the southwest bastion by storm. Until this moment our loss was trifle in number, being six or seven killed, and eighteen or twenty wounded.

Colonel Ledyard seeing the enemy within the fort, gave orders to cease firing and to throw down our arms, as the fort had surrendered. We did so, but they continued firing on us, crossed the fort and opened the gate, when they marched in, firing in platoons upon those retreating to the powder magazines and barracks-rooms for safety. At this moment the renegade Colonel Beckwith, commanding, cried out, "Who commands this garrison?" Colonel Ledyard, who was standing near me, answered, "I did sir, but you do now," at the same time stepping forward, handing him his sword with the point towards himself. At this instant I perceived a soldier in the act of bayoneting me from behind. I turned suddenly round and grasped his bayonet, endeavoring to unship it, and knock off the thrust, but in vain. Having but one hand, he succeeded in forcing it into my right hip, above the joint, and just below the abdomen, and crushed me to the ground. The first person I saw afterwards was my brave commander, a corpse by my side, having been run through the body with his own sword, by the savage renegade.[2]

The granite marker of the death of Major Montgomery on the grounds of Fort Griswold. *Courtesy of the Avery-Copp Museum–Jim Streeter Collection.*

Old powder house and monument, Fort Griswold, Groton, Connecticut. This card also represents a later time. *Courtesy of the Avery-Copp Museum–Jim Streeter Collection.*

The bronze gate marker at the entrance to Fort Griswold. *Photo by the author.*

Of the 165 defenders of the fort at the start of the battle, 88 men and boys were dead, 35 badly wounded and 28 taken prisoner, most of these slightly wounded. In addition, 13 escaped and one (twelve-year-old William Latham Jr.) was paroled. This information was taken from the bronze plaque on the memorial gates entrance to the park.

HEMPSTEAD CONTINUES

After the massacre they plundered us of everything we had, and left us literally naked. When they commenced gathering us up, together with their own wounded, they put theirs under the shade of the platform, and exposed us to the sun, in front of the barracks, where we remained over an hour. Those that could stand were the[n] paraded, and ordered to the landing, while those who could not (of which number I was one) were put in one of the ammunition wagons and were taken to the brow of the hill (which was very steep, and at least one hundred rods in descent), from whence it was permitted to run down by itself, but was arrested in its course, near the river, by an apple tree. The pain and anguish we endured in this rapid descent, as the wagon jumped and jostled over rocks and holes, is inconceivable; and the jar of its arrest was like bursting the cords of life asunder, and caused us to shriek with almost supernatural force. Our cries were distinctly heard and noticed on the opposite side of the river (which is a mile wide), amidst all the confusion which raged in the burning and sacking of the town. We remained in the wagon more than an hour before [our] humane conquerors hunted us up, when we were again paraded and laid on the beach preparatory to embarkation; but, by the interposition of Ebenezer Ledyard, brother to Colonel Ledyard, who humanely represented our deplorable situation and the impossibility of our being able to reach New York, thirty-five of us were paroled in the usual form. Being near the house of Ebenezer Avery, who was one of our number, we were taken into it. Here we had not long remained before a marauding party set fire to every room, evidently intending to burn us up with the house. The party soon left it, when it was with difficulty extinguished, and we were thus saved from the flames. Ebenezer Ledyard again interfered, and obtained a sentinel to remain and guard us until the last of the enemy embarked,—about 11 o'clock at night. None of our own people came to us till near daylight the next morning, not knowing previous to that time that the enemy had departed.

Such a night of distress and anguish was scarcely ever passed by mortal. Thirty-five of us were lying on the bare floor, stiff, mangled, and wounded in every manner, exhausted with pain, fatigue, and loss of blood, without clothes or anything to cover us, trembling with cold and spasms of extreme anguish without fire or light, parched with excruciating thirst, not a wound dressed, nor a soul to administer to one of our wants, nor an assisting hand to turn us during these long, tedious hours of the night. Nothing but groans and unavailing sighs were heard, and two of our number did not live to see the light of the morning, which brought with it some ministering angels to our relief. The first was in the person of Miss Fanny Ledyard of Southold, L.I., then on a visit to her uncle, our murdered commander, who held to my lips a cup of warm chocolate, and soon returned with wine and other refreshments, which revived us a little. For these kindnesses she has never ceased to receive my most grateful thanks, and fervent prayers for her felicity.

The cruelty of our enemy cannot be conceived, and our renegade countrymen surpassed in this respect, if possible our British foes. We were at least an hour after the battle within a few steps of a pump in the garrison, well supplied with water, and, although we were suffering with thirst, they would not permit us to take one drop of it, nor give us any themselves. Some of our number, who were not disabled from going to the pump, were repulsed with the bayonet; and not one drop did I taste after the action commenced, although begging for it after I was wounded of all who came near me.[3]

THE AFTERMATH

Prior to departing for New York, the British hastily buried their dead in shallow graves in the vicinity of the fort. Some years later, relatives of the dead returned to the site and recovered most of the bodies.

It is generally believed that spirits remain earthbound for one of several various reasons. Some are tied by love or affection for an individual who remains alive. For others, there is a love for a former place or activity. And for yet others, there can be a search for meaning, especially around old battlefields or accident sites. These individuals may be still seeking understanding—what happened, why did it happen and why were they left behind?

David Pitkin, author of *New England Ghosts*, had been invited to this historic area by a young man named James, who worked at the fort and had experienced strange events near the stone monument and museum. After interviewing James, David visited the old earthworks across the road:

> *Strolling among the old stonework base of the fort and the embankments atop them, I wondered just where Colonel William Ledyard had surrendered his sword to a British commander who then allegedly mortally stabbed the American commander with the weapon. Then I found the memorial stone, fenced for protection.*
>
> *I wandered through the parade ground to what appeared to be the old magazine, and then, as I returned northward toward the fort's gate, I asked myself whether all the spirits of the defenders had now left. Behind me I heard a voice say, "You'd be a fool to think so." I only half turned, as I knew nobody else was within the walls on this very hot August day.*[4]

In an effort to keep the history of the fort and the battle alive, the Friends of Fort Griswold hold an annual commemoration of the Battle of Groton Heights at the fort as close to the anniversary as possible. This normally occurs during Labor Day weekend. Sometimes, the group has have a reenactment or a short

The sally port, a small exit point in a fort through which troops pass, seen from the exterior of Fort Griswold. *Courtesy of the Avery-Copp Museum–Jim Streeter Collection.*

The granite marker where Colonel William Ledyard fell by his own sword on September 6, 1781. *Photo by the author.*

The protective fence erected around the marker where Colonel William Ledyard fell on September 6, 1781. *Courtesy of the Avery-Copp Museum–Jim Streeter Collection.*

Fort Griswold around the time of the War of 1812: *Courtesy of the Avery-Copp Museum–Jim Streeter Collection.*

Colonel William Ledyard's grave marker at the Colonel Ledyard Cemetery on Mitchell Street in Groton. The original grave stone is so deteriorated as to be unreadable and has a protective cover built over it. *Photo by Gerry Keeler.*

play to tell about the battle. The effort is to try to create different and interesting ways to inform the public about what happened on this site so many years ago.

A dream by one of the group's officers depicted a candlelight vigil to honor the dead, and at the 2011 commemoration, the Friends started utilizing that vision. Slightly before dusk, eighty-eight luminaries were lit to represent the eighty-eight defenders of the fort who died during and after the battle.

As the sun was setting over the ramparts in an orange sky, the names of the defenders killed were read by members of the Friends, and a candle was extinguished for each name called. The members reading the names were dressed in colonial garb—the women in long dresses and the men in period military uniform or civilian attire. An eerie wind picked up as darkness settled in. The group's vice-president had the following experience: "As I stood here in the evening light, for one brief moment, I felt the past touch me. It was like a wandering wind. They were with me in spirit, walking along the ramparts. This is a testament that they are still with us today, as they were on that fateful date in 1781."

During the ceremony, the audience members looked around as if they could feel something, but nothing was visible. After the ceremony, several in the audience spoke of a spooky feeling that someone was touching them. Others spoke of an eerie feeling coming over them as the names were called out. Still others spoke of how the vigil brought home the humanity of those who were killed and the enormity of the disaster.

My stepson, who is almost fifty, related to me an incident that happened many years ago. He and two friends, all of whom were teenagers at the time, were sitting on the ramparts of the fort one night. It was a moonless night, and as they sat talking, suddenly an eerie breeze blew across the fort; at the same time, all three felt something brush the backs of their heads. They turned to see what it was, but nothing was there. They were all terrified and ran out of the fort as fast as they could. It was a long time before they were able to go back into the fort at night.

Both visitors and paranormal investigators agree that the fort is a very haunted place. A shadowy figure has been seen in the sally port under the south wall of the fort, and disembodied voices can be heard. A man has been seen sitting about halfway up the stairs in the monument, but he disappears as he is approached. People have reported having stones tossed at them by unseen hands. An apparition in a tricorn hat has been seen at the gate in the north wall. Disembodied footsteps have been heard in the parade ground of the fort. Strange lights have been seen floating above the fort in the night air. There have also been reports of an unseen girl screaming, "No, no!"

SHIRLEYANNE'S STORY

My wife also has strong feelings about Fort Griswold and the surrounding area and has related the following experiences to me:

In 1978, as I sat on the landing of my new home, it was a bright, sunny, spring day. My furniture was arriving that day. I felt a sense of peace sitting on the stairs looking out the window as I waited for it to arrive. The trip from Pittsburgh to Groton had been tiring and I yearned to sleep in my own bed in my new home. My search for a house in Groton had been made in a hurry as my house in Pittsburgh had sold in less than two weeks of going on the market. A realtor in Groton had a list of houses ready for me to see. I looked at six houses and I had a number of "I could live in this house in a moment," but as I drove down my street, even before I saw the house, I knew I had found my new home. There was something that touched me and a voice in my head that said this is the place! When I saw the house, built in the late nineteenth century and full of New England charm, I was home. Soon I settled into my new life.

This house was a happy home, unlike the house I just left, so I felt happy about a new start in Groton. Six months went by quickly, and I started taking evening walks around Groton Bank. Each evening as I reached the foot of my street near the back entrance to Fort Griswold, I would feel that I wasn't alone. My dog Candy, a sweet Cocker Spaniel, would walk closer to me and keep looking back. I also looked behind me, thinking that someone must be walking behind us, but I saw no one. Winter came and went. Summer was wonderful, and I enjoyed my home and gardens. My evening walks were uneventful but enjoyable. In September, things changed again. My evening walks again made me feel as if someone was walking with us. Candy sensed it, too, and continually looked back.

I had experienced a ghostly presence in my last home; and I wondered if this could be similar. Could it be the spirit of someone who had lived in one of the houses on my street? I knew it didn't originate in my house, but there definitely was a presence. I didn't know the history of the area and didn't connect my experiences with the fort across the street. At this point, I didn't even walk in the fort. I believed it was just a place for kids to ride sleds in the winter and fly kites in the spring.

The next five years were busy ones. My walks stopped—the gym at work was more convenient and Candy had gone to live with my ex-husband. I felt guilty about skipping my walks and a voice inside me, especially in the fall, kept saying, "Walk." It seemed as if someone—or something—missed me and wanted me to resume my exploration of the neighborhood.

Up to this point, I had completely ignored the little library a few streets over. Then, one fall afternoon, I put my shoes on and went for a walk. As I approached the library and watched the Saturday visitors coming and going, I was drawn to this quaint, little building. As I reached for the door knob, it stuck for a second, and I half fell through the doorway. I couldn't believe my eyes; I felt like I had stepped back in time. The stone fireplace, the paintings and the marble busts perched on dark wooden shelves drew me in like a magnet. I was hooked. The front room, with its wing chairs, brick fireplace and a sword hanging above the mantel, was my favorite. I needed to know more. Who did this sword belong to? The library soon became my favorite destination on Saturday mornings. I started reading about Fort Griswold and the battle. Could there be a connection between the fort and my fall encounters? Could the presence I felt be a patriot on his way to defend the fort? Or was it one of Benedict Arnold's British soldiers? I needed answers.

I had no relatives living here at that time, nor did I know of any ancestors who had fought in the Revolutionary War. There was a family legend that an ancestor was the head scout for General Washington, but since this had never been proved, I quickly dismissed the notion of a family connection. The sword belonged to Colonel William Ledyard, who was killed with it in the hands of a British officer. I read with interest and horror of the carnage that followed on that September day in 1781. The British dead were buried in a shallow ditch within the fort.

After reading the account of the battle, I walked home alone thinking about what had happened on that fateful day. A breeze blew the fall leaves around my legs and a sudden chill came over me as I wondered to myself if the British dead were still trying to get home after the battle.

Today, thirty-eight years later, I still live in my old house in Groton Bank. I love living here and enjoy my walks with friends, my family and my dog of twelve years, Rosie. Do I still feel the presence in and near the fort? Yes! I am comfortable with the presence. Sometimes, when sitting in my upstairs bedroom window; on cold wintry nights, with the streetlights shining on the snow-covered street, I listen to the cold, northeast winds of New England. I tighten my blanket around me, and for a second, I see the shadowy figure of a sentry, bundled against the cold, still waiting to go home.

Are there still patriots or British soldiers roaming the ramparts of Fort Griswold? I leave it for you to decide. When I think of the eerie experiences that have been related to me and consider the reasons spirits stay behind, I tend to believe there are. They may be tied to events of the battle and its aftermath and the reasons behind those events. It is my opinion that if you believe they have all left, you could be mistaken.

2

The Mother Bailey House: Anna Warner Bailey

By Leslie Evans

Mother Bailey House, at the corner of Thames and Broad Streets in the city of Groton. This house served as a post office and tavern when Elijah and Anna Bailey lived here. *Photo by the author.*

Dr. Amos Prentice was the first owner of this house, which was built shortly after the Revolutionary War, replacing a structure that was burned during the British attack on New London Harbor in 1781. *Photo by the author.*

INTRODUCTION

A beautiful portrait of Anna Warner Bailey, sketched in 1834 when she was seventy-six years old, depicts a distinguished elderly lady wearing a white bonnet. What can this portrait tell us about "Mother Bailey"? She looks dignified and is nicely dressed, as befitted a person who was famous not only in her own town but also nationally and who was sitting for what was one of the few likenesses ever made of her during her lifetime. Having her portrait done would have been an important event in her life, and the result is beautiful; however, it doesn't reveal that she loved to dance and sing, that she was forthright and outspoken, that she was passionately patriotic and equally passionate in her hatred of all things British. This information is passed down through other sources, but on closer inspection of her portrait, there is a liveliness to her face and a sparkle in her eyes that gives a hint of her indomitable spirit. It was this strength of personality that carried her through some difficult early years, enabled her to weather tragedies, made

Portrait of Anna Warner Bailey. This portrait can be seen at the Monument House Museum on the grounds of Fort Griswold in Groton, Connecticut. *Courtesy of the Monument House Museum.*

her a leader in her community and drew people to enjoy the pleasure of her company. It also gave her the courage to act with boldness when called on to help in a wartime emergency, her actions drawing the attention of a wider public and bringing her a great deal of acclaim in her lifetime. An understanding of Mother Bailey's backstory and her courageous spirit is essential when pondering the possibility that something of her life force is still lingering in the house that was her home for so many years.

EARLY LIFE

Mother Bailey was born Anna Warner, in Groton, on October 11, 1758. Her father was Phillip Warner, who went to sea as a boy, often serving on ships that were based in New London Harbor. It was here that he met and married his wife, Hannah Mills. Phillip and Hannah Warner had been married only a few years and were the parents of two young children when Hannah contracted smallpox, from which she ultimately died. Phillip had been planning to leave on a sea voyage when his wife became ill. He postponed the trip in order to nurse her, and after her death, he set sail. He was not at sea long when he also developed smallpox, having been infected while caring for his wife. He did not survive and was buried at sea. Anna and her brother, now orphans, were taken into the custody of their grandmother Mills, who had married a second husband, James Starr. Their farm, on Candlewood Hill in the Center Groton area of town, was also the home of two uncles, James and Edward Mills.

REVOLUTIONARY WAR

Anna Warner's uncle Edward Mills was an ardent Patriot and a corporal in the local militia. During the early morning hours of September 6, 1781, when Benedict Arnold's invasion of New London began, the alarm guns sounded at Fort Griswold, calling the militia to rally to the protection of the fort. Edward Mills immediately left the family farm for the three-mile walk to Groton Heights, where he joined his commander, Colonel William Ledyard, in preparation to defend the fort against the oncoming British soldiers.

As the battle progressed, the sound of the cannons and musket fire could be heard some distance into the surrounding country. The rising smoke and the smell of the fire as New London and Groton burned were also evident to inland families, and although the fighting was over by midday, no immediate news of the outcome of the battle reached people who were not directly along the coast. Families anxiously awaited information and the hoped-for return of the men who had rallied to defend the fort. By evening, news had spread regarding the two towns being put to the torch, and the terrible reports came in of the garrison at Fort Griswold being overwhelmed by the much more numerous British troops. Most worrying were rumors that the defenders who survived the battle were put to the sword by the victorious

British. When Edward Mills did not return home and no word came of his fate, Anna Warner decided, early the next morning, to walk to Fort Griswold in an attempt to determine whether her uncle was dead or alive. She found him, badly wounded, in a house near the fort that had been converted into a makeshift hospital. Knowing that he was unlikely to survive his wounds and feeling himself getting weaker all the time, Edward Mills expressed a wish to see his wife and two young children, one of whom was a newborn. Anna immediately walked the three miles back to the family farm, saddled a horse for her aunt and the youngest baby and, carrying one child and leading the horse, again walked back to the fort. Her uncle was still alive when the family group arrived and was able to hold his children, but he died shortly afterward. His name is now engraved on the memorial monument at Fort Griswold, along with the other men who died there that day. This experience deeply scarred Anna Warner. The horror of the aftermath of the battle, the sight of so many of her former friends and neighbors lying dead, the horrible injuries inflicted on the dead and dying, the agony of the wounded survivors and the grief of family members—these were things she never forgot or forgave. Instead, she nurtured an almost fanatical hatred of all things British for the rest of her life.

TAVERN AND POST OFFICE

One of the soldiers who did survive the battle was a young man named Elijah Bailey. He had been wounded and taken away as a prisoner of war. After being held on a British prison ship in New York for a little over a month, he was paroled and returned to Groton. Conditions on the prison boat were horrific, with extremely high death rates due to overcrowding, lack of sanitation, poor quality of food and widespread disease. Several of the survivors of Fort Griswold died there; others returned to Connecticut in very poor health and died at home. Once he recovered from the ordeal, and after the war was over, Elijah Bailey married the young Anna Warner. Their marriage lasted sixty-five years, until his death at the age of ninety in 1848.

Several years after their marriage, Elijah Bailey was appointed postmaster of Groton, and the Baileys moved to a house beside the Thames River in the neighborhood known as Groton Bank. The house had been built after the Revolutionary War by Dr. Prentice, who had been one of the doctors who tended to the wounded after the Battle of Fort Griswold. Located just down the hill from Fort Griswold and very close to the landing site of the Groton–New London ferry, this house was well positioned to be a tavern and post office, a function it served during the many years that Elijah and Anna Bailey lived there. Anna's lively personality and the welcoming atmosphere that the tavern provided made this hostelry a popular spot for travelers seeking a meal and a bed and also for local men who gathered for a drink and to share the news with friends and neighbors. It was also a gathering place for everyone who came here to send or receive mail who kept Mother Bailey well informed about all the comings and goings in her village. She liked to be at the center of things, and her tavern and her husband's post office kept her at the hub of the Groton community. "Mother" was a courtesy title given to a woman who was well respected among her peers, and in the case of Anna Warner Bailey, it was purely honorary, as she never had any children of her own. She was, however, known to be very fond of neighborhood children and they of her. All were welcome at Mother Bailey's—young and old, friends and strangers—with one exception. British guests were not wanted at her tavern, and on the rare occasions when an English person stopped there by mistake, she made her feelings known. There is an old story of two English travelers, who, having heard of Mother Bailey, decided to try to trick her into serving them by pretending to be Scottish. She was not deceived, and they left in hurry.

WAR OF 1812, A SCARLET PETTICOAT AND FAME

Unlike many of her fellow citizens, many of whom depended financially on maritime commerce, Mother Bailey was very pleased when another war was declared against England in 1812. Never having mellowed in her hatred of the English, she was very vocal in her support of the war, and it was her fervent hope that the young United States would deal another blow to the British Empire.

The war would come very close to home during the summer of 1813. The American Navy squadron, led by Commodore Decatur, had been chased into New London Harbor by a superior British fleet, which then blockaded the mouth of the harbor, thwarting Decatur's escape and preventing any merchant ships from entering or leaving the port. A British attack on the area was thought to be imminent, and the garrison at Fort Griswold prepared to defend Groton. Many of the townspeople decided to evacuate to inland locations; the memory of the burning of New London and Groton after the last attack in 1781 was still fresh in the minds of many residents. Soldiers at the fort found themselves short of some necessary supplies, including flannel, which was needed as wadding material for the cannons. A man was sent out to acquire some in the surrounding neighborhood but met with little success, as many houses were vacant and the streets nearly deserted. One resident who had not evacuated was Mother Bailey. The soldier stopped her on the road in front of her house and explained his mission. She promptly reached inside her outer skirt and untied the red flannel petticoat that she wore underneath. Removing the petticoat right there in the street, she handed it over, accompanied by a fervent wish, in very strong language, that she hoped it would effectively serve to do its duty against the British. When the soldier returned to the fort with the petticoat and told the story of how he

Andrew Jackson by Thomas Sully, 1826. Mother Bailey had seven portraits of Andrew Jackson decorating the walls of her tavern: *Courtesy of the New York Public Library, Public Domain Digital Archives.*

A decorative cast-iron fence presented to Mother Bailey by Andrew Jackson. This fence was spared by the scrap metal drives during World War II that claimed almost all other decorative fencing in the neighborhood. *Photo by the author.*

acquired it, the garrison received the skirt with loud cheers and declared that instead of tearing it up for cannon wadding, they would attach it to a pike and fight under it, as a symbol of defiance. Fortunately for New London Harbor, the British squadron decided not to attack and, instead, turned its attention to Stonington, which was bombarded in August 1814.

The incident of Mother Bailey and her petticoat, which had been witnessed by people in the street and was widely reported by the soldiers, became a well-known story locally and found its way into the newspapers. Soon the story spread well beyond the local area, bringing Mother Bailey much notoriety; she reveled in her newfound fame as a loyal Patriot and enjoyed visits from many local dignitaries. As her story became nationally known, she was visited by Presidents James Monroe and Andrew Jackson and was entertained by the Marquis de Lafayette in New London when he toured America in 1824. Mother Bailey was particularly partial to Andrew Jackson; she had numerous portraits of him decorating her tavern. In front of her house can still be seen the remnants of an elegant cast-iron fence that he presented to her as a gift of thanks from the nation.

LATER YEARS

As time passed, Mother Bailey's fame did not diminish; in fact, she did much to keep her story alive. She was such an engaging personality and so loved to be the center of attention when telling her stories about both the revolution and the War of 1812 that people were naturally drawn to her. She was visited constantly over the next four decades by travelers, writers, artists and newspaper reporters. Her portrait was painted during her lifetime and is now displayed at the Monument House Museum at Fort Griswold. Her portrait was also drawn by John Warner Barber when he traveled through Groton in 1835. She lived long enough to come into the age of photography as well and had her likeness taken in old age.

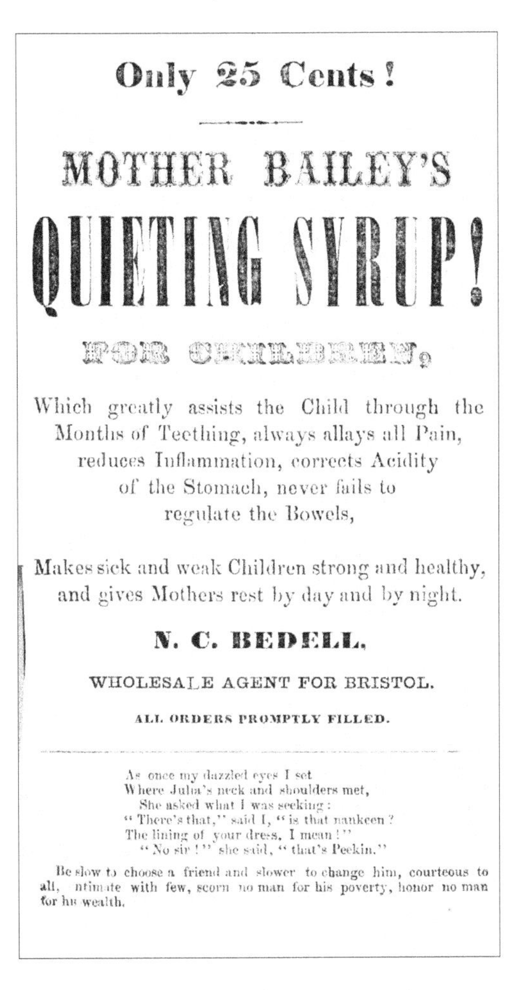

Mother Bailey's Quieting Syrup, a narcotic sedative that was very popular for many years in the mid-nineteenth century. Mother Bailey did not manufacture this syrup; her famous name was used as an endorsement to increase sales. *Courtesy of the Avery-Copp Museum archive.*

Mother Bailey was a celebrity in her own time. As is still the practice, well-known people sometimes leant their name or likeness as an endorsement of various commercial products. In the case of Anna Warner Bailey, it was *Mother Bailey's Quieting Syrup*, an opium-based concoction designed for "quieting" restless children, which it undoubtedly did in an age when the dangers of such drugs were not yet recognized.

Mother Bailey aged remarkably well at a time when there were many obstacles to a long life. She maintained excellent health and physical energy well into her eighties, often surprising guests by jumping up and dancing a jig if the mood struck her, and never required the use of eyeglasses for reading or needlework. She began to slow down only after the death of her husband, who had been her constant companion for over six decades. His loss affected her joyful spirit, but her physical health and mental capacity were not diminished. She often announced her intent to live to be one hundred, and in all likelihood would have done so had she not suffered a terrible accident in her home when she was ninety-three years old. Fire, always a danger in wooden homes heated by fireplaces and illuminated by candlelight, was the cause of her misfortune. Sitting alone after her midday dinner in a comfortable armchair in front of her bedchamber fireplace and perhaps seeking warmth on a cold January day, she drew her chair a little too near the flames. Her dress caught fire, and Mother Bailey suffered serious burns. The fire in the room, which had spread to her carpet and her chair, was soon extinguished, but her injuries were so severe that she died within the hour, on January 10, 1851. Her friends and family were devastated by this tragic end to such a vibrant and well-loved member of the community. Mother Bailey was laid to rest beside her husband at the Starr Hill Burying Ground in Groton and surrounded by the graves of many of the childhood friends that she had outlived.

HAUNTED HAPPENINGS

After the death of Mother Bailey, her house passed into the care of other owners, and it changed hands on a fairly regular basis over the years. Alterations happened in the surrounding neighborhood, too, as the Civil War saw many young men from Groton and nearby towns march off to fight for the Union cause. After the war, the economy of the area underwent some significant changes, with the decline of the whaling industry and the introduction of new forms of commerce. The road in front of Mother Bailey's old house was still an important commercial area, now known as Thames Street, and home to many small businesses, such as grocers, coal merchants, livery stables, a cobbler, hardware store, fish market and even a banjo factory. The ferry landing moved a few blocks south, steamships replaced sail in the harbor, and the coming of the railroad, followed by the trolley, opened up new options for transportation. The face of the neighborhood changed as well; families descended from the original colonists still predominated well into the twentieth century, but they were living side by side with new

The fireplace in the old kitchen of the Mother Bailey House. *Photo by the author.*

immigrants from Ireland and Italy. As new families came and went, the old Bailey House saw an ever-changing cast of characters. At the best of times, the house was loved and well cared for, but there were other years when this venerable old home stood vacant. Whether occupied or empty, there was always one constant: Mother Bailey's spirit does not seem to have ever left.

There are old stories spanning the past century, when the house had long since ceased to serve as an inn, that tell of some sort of unexplained "tavern" activities taking place there. Passersby would report the sounds of cards being shuffled, tankards clinking and conversation and laughter emanating from the house, usually late at night. Some people avoided walking past there for this reason, but most neighbors seemed to accept it as an idiosyncrasy of the place; some even walked that way in the hope of hearing the ghostly sounds. One Groton resident reported that as a teenager during the early 1950s, he and some friends sneaked into the house at night during one of the periods when it was unoccupied. They explored the empty house, especially interested to see if they could find traces of the opening of a tunnel reputed to be in the cellar and said to have once been used by smugglers. The opening was still there; however, the tunnel had been filled in, so they were

The staircase leading from the entry hall to the second floor of the Mother Bailey House. *Photo by the author.*

unable to explore farther. Instead, they decided to investigate the attic. It was while they were up on the third floor that they became aware of the tavern noises from downstairs, especially the sound of cards shuffling, indistinct conversation and what they thought was fiddle music. Too frightened to go back down, they waited for hours in the attic until long after any sounds downstairs had died away. When morning light began to show in the sky, they made a dash down the two flights of stairs and out the back door.

A more recent story about the house was kindly shared by a lady whose father lived there in the late 1970s. He shared the house with a group of roommates, all young men stationed at the naval submarine base a few miles north on the Thames River. These men were very aware of what they described as a "presence" in the house, but they never felt frightened or threatened by it; it was just part of the atmosphere. This changed when one of the housemates began dating a young English lady who had recently moved to the United States. She always felt uneasy in the house and several times mentioned that she felt a chill or a draft that was not noticeable to others. One night, after a late outing, she decided to sleep over, but she did not last the night. Something happened that frightened her so much that it caused her to run outside, screaming, in the middle of the night. She would not describe the incident, but nothing would convince her to go back inside. Possibly Mother Bailey did not like the idea of an English guest, even a female one, two hundred years after the revolution.

Perhaps the most compelling story about the Mother Bailey House relates an incident that took place only a few years ago. The lovely old house had entered into some of its darkest days, owned by an absentee landlord, suffering from lack of maintenance and some unfortunate alterations while short-term renters moved in and out. The City of Groton, concerned about the fate of a structure that is such an important part of local history, purchased the house with the intent of ultimately restoring it. Shortly after the purchase, two city employees were looking over the house to plan future maintenance, and on the day in question, they were inspecting and photographing conditions in the cellar. The cellar is a full basement, about eight feet deep, with stone walls and a dirt floor. It contains a massive granite fireplace and was probably used as a kitchen in the eighteenth-century tavern days. There is also an arched opening, lined with brick, that appears to be the entrance of an old tunnel or the foundation of a former chimney, long since removed. The arch is about six feet high, and the opening extends back under the house for perhaps ten feet. The cellar contains a network of modern pipes and metal ductwork for the heating system juxtaposed against the historic stonework. During the inspection, one man was standing on the stairs while the other began photographing the basement. As he turned to change direction, he noticed a figure out of the corner of his eye. Startled, he paused to look and saw the distinct image of a man wearing what appeared to be clothing from the time of the Revolutionary War, with a knapsack slung across his back. He was leaning against the arched opening of the tunnel in a relaxed posture, much as someone might do when pausing for a rest or to talk with friends. Both of the men saw the image, which was transparent rather than solid, and the one who was taking pictures actually photographed it. Although the cellphone picture was not of a quality to be able to reproduce it in this book, it was clear enough, combined with the visual image of what they had just seen, to allow the two men to do some investigating to try to determine what time period the apparition might be from. Based on the style of his coat, breeches, his tricorn hat and the buttons on the coat, they determined that he was from the late eighteenth or early nineteenth century. In addition to his knapsack, the time-traveling visitor had a leather sack on his belt. This turned out to be a cartridge pouch, which would have been used to hold musket balls, indicating that he was, indeed, a soldier. There was no interaction between the ghostly image and the people observing him, nor did there seem to be any awareness on his part of the modern visitors; it was as if he just slipped out of time for a moment, allowing two twenty-first-century men to glimpse a moment in time from two centuries ago.

Modern ghost hunting technology has also paid a visit to the Mother Bailey House. Thames Society of Paranormal Investigations (TSPI) conducted research here in the early summer of 2014. The scope of their work includes measuring for sound, temperature, movement and electrical fields inside the building. Their findings were varied, with some interesting observations. Visually, there was only one incident reported, which was a shadowy figure that appeared for just a few seconds in a corner of the basement. Sounds were recorded, and although they seemed to be speech patterns, words were not distinguishable. The exceptions were a male voice saying, "I will" quite clearly and a female voice that responded twice to questions posed by the investigators. When they asked, "Are you here, Anna?" a voice distinctly replied, "I'm here," and when they asked if she would talk about the petticoat story, it sounds as if the response is "You're crazy."

A medium was also present during the investigation. In order to keep her opinions impartial, she was not told of any background information regarding Mother Bailey or the house. Nevertheless, the medium stated that there was an elderly woman in the building who made it clear that this was her house and that she ran things in the home. Although free to roam about the house at will, the spirit tended to favor one of the upstairs bedchambers. The medium also reported the presence of two small children in the house who moved around constantly during the investigation, mostly on the ground floor. It is not known who these children might be, but certainly many families have lived here over the years. The paranormal investigators concluded that the house is spiritually active and noted that there are two factors that might contribute to that circumstance. Buildings that have served as inns or taverns tend to have a high degree of paranormal activity reported, as do sites where someone has suffered a traumatic injury or death. These are both characteristics of the Mother Bailey House.

LINGERING SPIRITS

So what can we say with certainty about Anna Warner Bailey? There are many strong words that might describe her: resolute, determined, stubborn, steadfast, tough, staunch, unwavering. She loved her family and her friends, and she loved to be the center of attention. She was a good neighbor and a good citizen who lived through some exciting and tumultuous times in our nation's history. Pleased with her fame during her lifetime, she would probably be very pleased with the way she has been memorialized since her death. A ballad, very popular in its day, was written to commemorate her shortly after she died. At the turn of the last century, the Anna Warner Bailey Chapter of the Daughters of the American Revolution was formed in Groton and is still active in promoting historic preservation in the area. Mother Bailey's image has decorated numerous souvenirs over the years, and many of these are still much sought after by collectors. Most of all, she is probably quite pleased that an effort is being made to save her old home, where it seems she is still very much in residence. With a spirit as strong as Anna Warner Bailey's, maybe even death can't keep her down.

Mother Bailey commemorative china, circa 1900. This china was commissioned by the Anna Warner Bailey Chapter of the Daughters of the American Revolution. *Photo by the author.*

3

The Avery–Copp House: If These Walls Could Talk

By Leslie Evans

This is not a quiet house. Floors creak, radiators hiss, pipes gurgle and thump, wind whistles around chimneys, windows rattle, doors squeak, clocks tick—but it is much quieter now, in its recent life as a historic house museum, than it was as the residence of the Avery and Copp families in centuries past. For two hundred years, six generations of mothers, fathers, brothers, sisters and grandparents called this house "home." At any one time, the family in residence was supplemented by nieces and nephews, aunts and uncles and family friends who enjoyed extended stays here during transitional periods in their lives. Irish immigrant domestic servants worked in this house from the middle of the nineteenth century until the 1920s and were an important part of the household. Finally, there were family pets—dogs large and small, cats and their kittens and outdoor animals, such as chickens and horses. The house was alive with the sounds and activities of family life because before it was a museum, it was a home. This is something to keep in mind as we explore its history and that of its families and as we consider some of the spiritual associations and unexplained occurrences associated with this building over the years.

The Avery-Copp House, built circa 1800, on Thames Street in Groton, Connecticut. *Photo by the author.*

HISTORY OF THE HOUSE

The Avery-Copp House is located in the area of Groton that attracted the earliest colonial settlement; it was known as Groton Bank, and the riverbank in front of the Avery-Copp House was the site of the earliest ferry landing on the east side of the Thames River. Cary Latham, who had charge of the first ferry, built a house near here in 1655. His great-great-grandson Latham Avery moved into a relatively new house nearby in the 1820s, and this structure is the one we know today as the Avery-Copp House. The house had been built by Latham's cousin, Rufus Avery, shortly after the Revolutionary War. By the time Latham Avery purchased the house, New London and Groton had begun to recover from the economic devastation and personal loss wrought by the revolution on this area. The harbor had become a center of commercial and maritime activity, and Latham Avery himself had prospered, going to sea as a young man and making his fortune in maritime trade. Many of his neighbors were sea captains or successful merchants who built fashionable homes as an expression of their newfound prosperity.

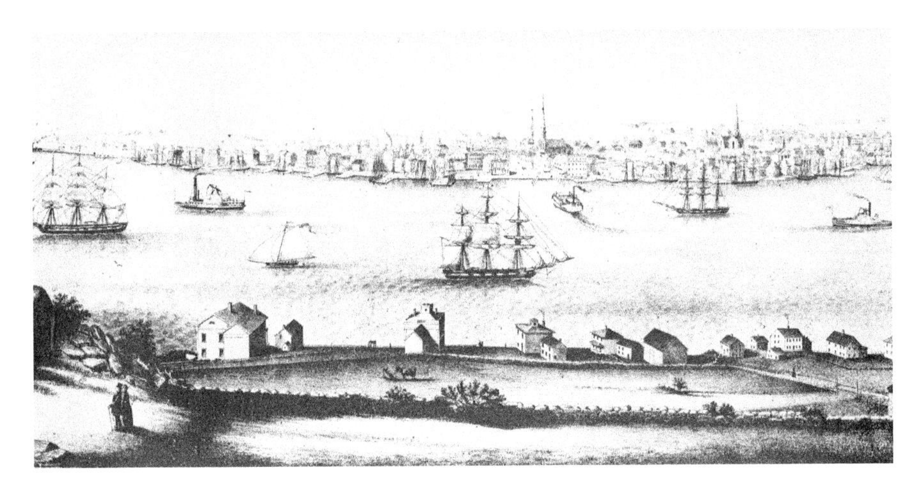

View of New London, 1857. This scene depicts New London Harbor at a transitional time between the great age of sail and the coming of the steam ship. E.C. Kellogg, Hartford, Connecticut. *Courtesy of the Avery-Copp Museum archives.*

Latham Avery and his young bride, Betsey Wood Lester, raised seven children in this house—two boys and five girls. Their eldest son, also named Latham, followed his father to sea but died in Hong Kong as a young man. Most of the other children married and raised families of their own in other houses. Two of the daughters, Mary Jane and Deborah, stayed on in the same house where they had been born, living here for the rest of their lives.

Mary Jane married Albert Ramsdell, a successful banker, and he moved into the family home. At this point, Mary Jane started to make some changes to the house. She is the one person, in all the generations living here, who didn't seem to mind extravagant expenses when it came to decorating her home, and she set about changing what had been a traditional colonial-style center chimney house into a home that reflected her Victorian tastes. Mary Jane is the one who added porches and bay windows, dormers and gingerbread trim, extravagant wallpapers, marble fireplace mantels and decorative wood floors. She had a special china cabinet built to hold a large set of rose-medallion porcelain that her brother Latham brought home to her from the Far East. (It is still there—every piece). Mary Jane decorated the house with gilded mirrors, oil paintings and decorative objects from around the world, but she did not discard her father's desk or his tall case clock; she added much that was new while keeping the old. Mary Jane and Albert Ramsdell entertained frequently, and this house was a local center of social life and family gatherings.

Avery-Copp House parlor, circa 1880. Most of the furniture and decorative objects in this picture are still in the room today. *Courtesy of the Avery-Copp Museum archives.*

Mary Jane and Albert did not have children of their own, and when they died, Mary Jane's younger sister Deborah inherited the house. Not having married until middle age, Deborah did not have children either. She had considered leaving her property to the Town of Groton as a public park, but in the end, she passed the family home (and her dog) on to her favorite niece, Betsey Avery, and to Betsey's husband, Belton Allyn Copp.

Betsey and Belton Copp moved here in 1895 and raised their three children in this house: Allyn, Emily and Joe. Allyn and Emily married and raised families of their own, but Joe remained a bachelor. When his parents grew older and began to suffer health problems, Joe Copp moved back home to help care for them. Betsey and Belton Copp both passed away in 1930, but Joe stayed on in the house, alone except for his housekeeper. Joe combined the traits of sentimentality and Yankee frugality to an extreme degree, making a concerted effort to keep the house just as his parents had left it. If something wore out, he would have it replaced just as it had been before. He did not like to have furniture rearranged or decorative objects moved around, and in keeping with his frugal nature, he threw nothing away if there was any possibility that the object might be of use in the future. These traits, although a boon to historians coming after him, must have made his housekeeper's life difficult at times. In the 1960s, Joe shocked his family when, at the age of seventy-two, he made the decision to marry his widowed second-cousin Mary. He did not allow Mary to live in his family home, as he did not want her to make any changes to the house. Instead, they lived in her home, and he would come to the Avery-Copp House every day to check on things, to read his mail and to do his paperwork. Joe and Mary lived very long lives, celebrating their twenty-fifth wedding anniversary. Joe Copp died in 1991 at the age of 101, and Mary died a few years later at 104. Because Joe had no children, his property passed to the children of his brother and sister. It was these nieces and nephews, the great-great-grandchildren of Latham Avery, who decided to preserve the old family home by opening it to the public as a historic house museum.

Joseph Copp (1889–1991), Yale class of 1911. *Courtesy of the Avery-Copp Museum archives.*

The Avery and Copp families would have known all the triumphs and tragedies common to the human experience, and because generation after generation lived here, many of these stories were played out within the walls of this house. There was joy—courtships and marriages in the parlor, babies born in the bedrooms upstairs, children growing up here among family and friends and young adults going off to seek their fortunes at sea, joining the navy or going to college. There were sorrows, too—women who died in childbirth, children with lives cut short by sickness and men lost at sea or as casualties of war. There was change—new beginnings for immigrants seeking refuge from the hunger and political turmoil in their Irish homeland and new brides coming to make their mark on the house where they would raise a new generation of children. And there was continuity—long and happy marriages, one generation handing the house over to the next, family members passing away in the same room in which they had been born and having their funeral conducted in the same parlor where their christening party had been held.

In the course of all this personal change, the house itself stood firm, surviving the destruction of hurricanes and the dangers of war. The neighborhood changed around it, and society changed too, as the automobile took over from the horse and carriage, the trolley and ferry passed out of use and the street in front of the house was paved. Inside, there were changes as well, most importantly the introduction of electricity and indoor plumbing. The piano was replaced by the radio, the icebox by the refrigerator, the telegraph by the telephone. Some things did not change though—the family habit of saving everything and wasting nothing, of preserving the character of their home for the next generation, of adding something new but never taking anything out. After six generations, this resulted in a house full of objects that tell the stories of all the people who have called this place home; it is a time

The landscape at the Avery-Copp House, circa 1885. *Courtesy of the Avery-Copp Museum archives.*

capsule of domestic life in a New England seaport town. People came and went, one generation passed on to the next, but through it all, the house was the one constant.

SPIRITS STILL WITH US

Perhaps it is not so surprising that some of the souls who found this house to be a haven during their lifetimes seem to be reluctant to leave it. Stories passed down in families, shared by neighbors and related by people who have visited the house in recent years make us wonder whose spirit may be lingering here. There are very possibly many more stories than the ones we know about now, as we are unable to talk to prior residents, now deceased, such as Joe Copp and his two housekeepers. Fortunately, ghost stories are memorable, and from time to time, a visitor to the house will relate an incident that they heard about from an elderly relative. The following stories raise more questions than answers, but are interesting just the same.

The north side of the Avery-Copp House contains windows that open onto the parlor and library on the first floor, two family bedrooms on the second floor and a servant's bedroom on the third, or attic, level. The neighboring house on this side is an eighteenth-century home built by the same Rufus Avery who once owned the Avery-Copp House. Over the years, various families have occupied that house, with the current owners having been there for a number of years. Since at least the 1940s, all of these families, whether their tenure was long or short, have reported seeing "figures" or "apparitions" in one or another of these north-facing windows. Stories might go back further than the early 1940s, but we have not been able to speak to anyone who lived in the house prior to that time. All reports are very similar and involve a figure that appears to be female. The figure and its clothing is described as being of a filmy white shade but not transparent. This image is most often reported at one of the second-floor bedroom windows, but all floors have had occurrences. There is never any facial or costume detail visible, which would help us to identify an era in time. So many ladies have lived in this house over the past two centuries that it is impossible to guess who the figure might represent or whether it is only one person. These sightings have been reported at all hours of the night but just as often at twilight. One elderly lady, interviewed in 2001, had spent her childhood in the Rufus Avery House. The family bathroom faces the Avery-

The bay window on the north side of the Avery-Copp House, a site favored by "the lady in white." *Photo by the author.*

Copp House, and she related that if someone had to use the bathroom at night, they would naturally have a view of the neighboring building. It was not unusual, in the morning over breakfast, for someone to say, "I saw the white lady last night."

The second floor of the house contains four bedrooms—three large and one small—and a bathroom. At the top of the curved stairway that comes up from the first floor, there is a large landing that serves as a reading area with a chaise lounge, a desk and bookcases. There is also a long hallway running along the back of the house, leading from bedrooms to bathroom. Off this hallway, the back stairs go down to the kitchen and up to the servant's quarters in the attic. The next unexplained occurrence involves the small bedroom, which opens onto the long back hall. This story was related to us by a man who was a guest in the house in the 1980s. He was sleeping in this bedroom and was roused from sleep by the sound of someone walking in the hall. He thought the footsteps belonged to the housekeeper, who was still living in the house at that time, and he wondered why she was walking around in the middle of the night. As the steps approached his open door, the

The second-floor hallway. The servant's staircase to the third floor opens off this hall. *Photo by the author.*

sound stopped, but no one walked past the room. He looked into the hall, but no one was there. Thinking it was perhaps his imagination, he went back to bed but could not fall asleep. After a short time, he heard the footsteps again, but this time, he was too frightened to get up and look into the hall. The footsteps were a louder, firmer tread the second time, and instead of stopping, they passed right by the door. In the morning, he questioned the housekeeper, but she said she knew nothing about it and had definitely not come downstairs during the night.

Another story involves this same floor of the house but took place in a bedroom situated in the northeast corner of the building. Historically, this room was used by various family members and other guests who stayed in the house. People tended to pay extended visits in the years when travel was difficult; having visitors for a month or more was not unusual. There are also instances of relatives who came to stay here while going through periods of transition in their lives, including a woman who had been recently widowed, an elderly couple who had suffered financial setbacks and an orphaned teenage girl who was a niece of Mary Jane Ramsdell. This room was generally a hospitable, comfortable haven, but in one instance, a guest was made to feel distinctly unwelcome. A young woman sleeping in this room awoke during the night with an uneasy feeling. As her eyes adjusted to the darkness, she became aware of a figure standing beside her bed. He was a middle-aged man, dressed in what she described as "old-fashioned" clothing, including a black hat. The man stood with hands on hips, looking down at her with what she interpreted as an annoyed expression, as if he disapproved of her being there, and radiated a hostile attitude. He did not

The northeast bedroom, apparently haunted by a gentleman from the nineteenth century. *Photo by the author.*

move or speak but appeared to be of solid form, not at all transparent or wispy. She felt frozen with fear, unable to move or scream. They looked at each other for what felt like a very long time but was probably less than a minute; she then closed her eyes in the hope of blocking out the image. When she opened her eyes, he was gone.

A very recent and intriguing incident was experienced several times over the past two years by one of the Avery-Copp Museum staff members and writer in residence, Joanie DiMartino. It is best to let Joanie share this story in her own words, beginning with a very appropriate quote.

JOANIE DIMARTINO

I wouldn't give a hoot for anybody who doesn't believe in ghosts.
—Reverend Dr. W.A.R. Goodwin, Colonial Williamsburg visionary and founder, to newspaper columnist Ernie Pyle, 1936

During my first summer as an interpreter at the Avery-Copp House, I had a strong, disconcerting sensation of being followed from room to room as I opened the museum each morning and closed up each afternoon. It's difficult to explain because I didn't actually see anything or hear noises other than usual ones—water pipes working, windows rattling on occasion from the breeze off the river—but felt more of a presence, that sense you get when you feel you're not alone, even though I was the first person in and the last person out on those days. Often we tell ourselves that such sensations are our vivid imaginations at work, but it was so compelling at times that I'd find myself glancing over my shoulder, especially when opening or closing up the second and third floors. I wondered if it wasn't one of the Irish servants who used to work and live in the house at the turn of the twentieth century keeping an eye on me from beyond, making certain I was caring for the house properly, or maybe a member of the Copp family doing the same from long ago. Imagining the presence I had felt as a former resident of the house overseeing my work was comforting, in part because the impression I felt wasn't negative—I would describe it as stern. After my first summer there, I no longer felt a distinctive presence alongside me as I performed my duties. That may be because I was no longer new—the entity or entities in the house approved: I had passed muster!

So the house to me felt like an ordinary, empty museum one bright morning in June as I arrived to prepare for tours at the beginning of another summer season. I unlocked the door, turned off the alarm and began turning on lights and pulling up shades. When I entered the sitting room, however, I caught the unmistakable scent of cigarette smoke. My first thought was one of concern—had someone been smoking recently in the museum, or was it possible the scent exuded from an artifact in the room? I finished preparing the museum for tours and went back to the sitting room. This first-floor room was the place where staff would peruse research books or work on projects in between giving tours. I could still smell cigarette smoke, so I walked around the room—sniffing couch fabric, pillows, books—trying to figure out where the smell was coming from so I could inform the director if an artifact might need further cleaning or care. The windows in this room do not open, so it wasn't possible that the smell could have blown into the house from a passerby smoking on the sidewalk. The scent was located in the far left corner of the room, by the entry to the dining room. It lingered in the air near a rocking chair next to the fireplace, but I couldn't connect it with any single item in that small area. I made a note to talk to the director about it on Monday and then prepared to work on my poetry collection and await visitors. Shortly afterward, I went to make a cup of tea, and when I walked by the same corner of the room, the cigarette fragrance was gone! It must have been no more than fifteen or twenty minutes since I arrived, but I could smell no trace of cigarette smoke in the sitting room or anywhere else in the museum.

There is a belief among paranormal specialists that some hauntings are by "perfume ghosts." A "perfume ghost" is a spirit or entity that haunts by leaving a trace of odor instead of other anomalies typical of hauntings, such as the sound of footsteps heard in an empty hall or apparitions. The aroma of a "perfume ghost" can be of anything—baking bread, fresh roses, a special fragrance. The last is often mentioned by people who have the unexpected—yet comforting—experience of smelling the favorite perfume worn by a deceased loved one. Sometimes, the same fragrance will move from room to room, detectable, for example, at one time in the kitchen and at another in a bedroom. At times, it occurs repeatedly in the same location, as I experienced with the cigarette odor that summer. It was not apparent every single day I worked, but frequently, I'd find myself walking past an abrupt scent of cigarette. The scent was always in the sitting room as I readied for my day, and as occurred the first time I smelled the smoke aroma, it lingered in the room for no more than fifteen minutes after I arrived. I began to feel disappointed on the days I'd open the house and the smell was absent!

Later that summer, when I mentioned my experiences to the director, she recalled that it was in the sitting room where Joe Copp, the last member of the Copp family to reside in the house, would regularly take his morning coffee, read the paper and, yes, smoke cigarettes. So it's possible that this was another way the ghosts in the house let me know that they were keeping an eye on me. Or maybe in opening up the museum I'd interrupted Joe's routine—still kept on Saturday mornings, long past his death.

Paranormal Investigation

The Thames Society of Paranormal Investigation (TSPI) visited the Avery-Copp House in the spring of 2012 with the purpose of conducting an objective investigation at the museum. We were impressed with the high degree of professionalism and respect that this group demonstrated; it did not seem that they were seeking to sensationalize or exploit any spirits that might be in the house or put a paranormal slant on occurrences that might have other explanations. This type of investigation seeks to research paranormal activity using tangible, measurable results. Measurable results might be generated by sound and measured as electronic voice phenomena (EVP). Other results may be visual and documented by photography, either motion or still images. Temperature changes within a room are also recorded, and motion sensors seek to record activity that cannot be documented visually.

The "white lady" so often reported at the windows did not make herself known during this investigation. The footsteps in the hall did seem to be active though; one of the investigators was on the third floor and clearly heard someone walking in the hallway on the floor below. She was the only person in the area at the time, and although she investigated, she could not find a source for the footsteps. In response to her questioning, she believes that she heard a male voice say, "It's me" but was unable to elicit any further response.

The only manifestation that was captured visually happened on the third floor. The lead investigator saw a strange mist, dark in color, which appeared suddenly and then dissipated as it moved under a closed door. This was documented on a video recorder. The third floor was also the location of one of the audio responses that were recorded that night. The lead investigator, knowing that the servants who lived in these attic rooms were Irish immigrants, asked some questions about their decision to come to America. When he asked if some of them left Ireland because of the Great

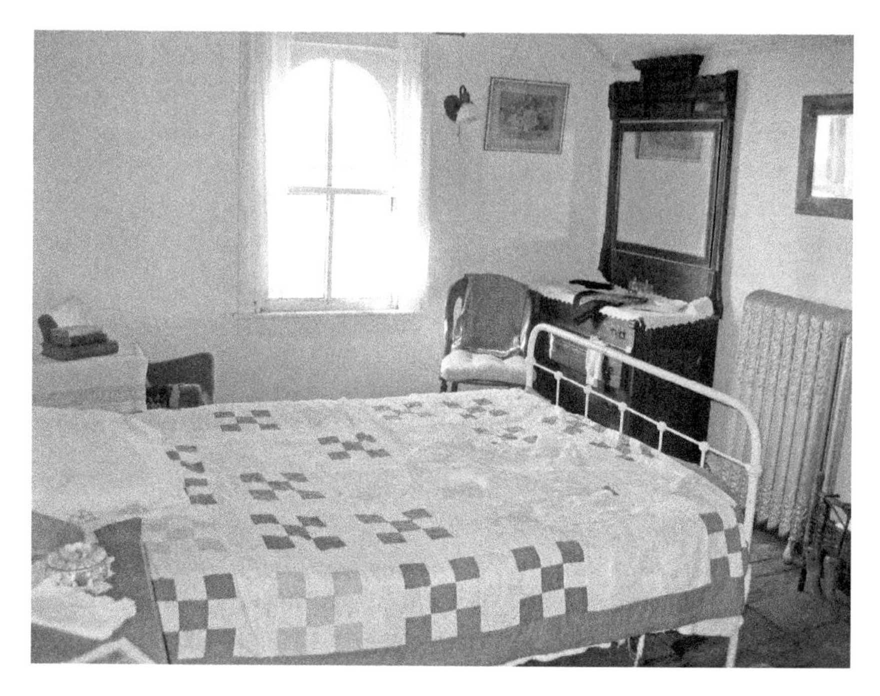

The housekeeper's bedroom, in the third-floor servants' quarters. *Photo by the author.*

The historic kitchen at the Avery-Copp House. *Photo by the author.*

Hunger (or the Irish potato famine), he heard a response that sounded like "Aye" or something similar to that. Another electronic voice phenomenon recorded in the house occurred in the sitting room, where a voice was heard to say, "They can see us." This recording is fairly garbled and has a great deal of static; it is not possible to tell if the voice is male or female.

In the kitchen, one of the investigators felt he was getting audio responses to his questions, but they were best described as whispers and did not show up on recordings. During the course of their visit, the Thames Society of Paranormal Investigation concluded that the house definitely is spiritually active. Activity tended to come in short bursts and be centered, for the most part, on the kitchen area and on the third floor, but various phenomena manifested themselves throughout the house. The investigators explained that results can vary considerably based on environmental conditions and time of year. Being located close to the water (we are beside the Thames River) can also impact the way energy is conducted and help to fuel paranormal events. Perhaps someday we will have a second investigation and see if we can add to our knowledge of the spirits who dwell here.

THE LAST WORD

In conclusion, yes, there are ghost stories here, but stronger than anything else is a feeling of not being alone in this house, of a presence of the past that goes beyond the physical objects inside and the old structure that surrounds them. These walls can, indeed, talk. If you listen, you can almost hear the laughter in the next room, a dog barking, teacups clinking against saucers, children at their play, pots clattering in the kitchen, the clock striking the hour. But wait! The clock is real. It is the same clock that was striking the hour for Latham Avery when this house was new, and the same clock that has marked the hours for all his descendants and their extended families over the generations. Perhaps the ghostly presence here is not strange at all but is, instead, the most natural thing in an old house that has shared so much of life with the people who have inhabited it over the years. We are definitely not alone here.

4

The Bill Memorial Library: No Smoking, Please!

By Hali Keeler

On a rise overlooking the Thames River in Groton sits a beautiful stone building surrounded by grassy lawns: the Bill Memorial Library (BML). Although often mistaken for an H.H. Richardson building, it was actually designed by architect Stephen Earle of Worcester, Massachusetts. It is constructed of Stony Creek granite and trimmed with Maynard freestone.

The original Bill Memorial Library in 1890, designed by Stephen Earle in the style of H.H. Richardson. *Photo from author's collection.*

The library was founded by Frederic Bill and given to the people of Groton in 1888, but the building was not constructed until 1890. Until that time, the collection resided in a room of the Groton Heights Elementary School next door. This was the first library in Groton, and Mr. Bill gave it in memory of his sisters, Eliza and Harriet, both of whom died in their teens. These are the first deaths to be associated with this building.

WHO WAS FREDERIC BILL?

His family dates back to 1638, when John and Dorothie Bill immigrated to Boston from England. Around 1668, Philip Bill, a descendant of this branch of the family, was summoned to Groton, ostensibly at the behest of Governor John Winthrop Jr. of New London. Frederic, a seventh-generation descendant, was one of several children born to Gurdon and Lucy (Yerrington) Bill of what was then known as North Groton. The children included Edward, twins Henry and Joshua, Joseph, Gurdon, Frederic, Eliza, Frederic, Ledyard, Harriet and Charles. There were two sons named Frederic; the first was born in 1829 and lived only one year. "Our" Frederic was more fortunate; he was born on September 7, 1833, and lived eighty-seven years, until April 2, 1920. Siblings Joshua and Joseph also died in infancy. It is interesting to note that Gurdon Sr. served as a representative to the state legislature at the time that North Groton separated from Groton and became its own town. The new town was named Ledyard for Colonel William Ledyard, who led the American troops in the Battle of Groton Heights during the Revolutionary War, and Gurdon was given the honor of naming his newborn son after the new town.

Frederic's two sisters also died young—Eliza at age sixteen and Harriet at age nineteen. While no cause of death is ascribed to Harriet, it is noted in the family genealogy that Eliza succumbed to typhoid fever. The library has Harriet's last will and testament, handwritten by someone other than herself; it is noted near the signature that she was so weak that she could barely sign it. The will is poignant, as she bequeaths items to her siblings and others, including a silver spoon, a shawl and copies of her daguerreotype. The will is preserved in the Bill Memorial's archives.

Frederic Bill took a circuitous path in life. He attended Roberts' Academy in the nearby village of Poquetanuck before continuing his studies at Suffield Literary Institute in Suffield, Connecticut. At age sixteen, he was back on the family farm and teaching at the Lestertown District School in Ledyard. Apparently Frederic desired a more active life, since he subsequently embarked on a trip to the British Provinces, visiting Canada, including New Brunswick and Nova Scotia, as well as the southern and western United States while selling books.[5] He returned in 1856 to partner with his brother in the publishing house of Gurdon Bill in Springfield, Massachusetts.[6] (It must have been preordained that he would create a public library.) By the winter of 1857–58, he was on the road again, this time to Cuba aboard the vessel *Black Warrior*. He spent several weeks there observing the local customs and enjoying the "luxurious fruits and charming landscapes."[7]

Upon his return, he married Lucy Glover Denison in May 1858. At the outbreak of the Civil War in 1861, he retired from trade, sold his interest in his brother's publishing business and traveled with his wife through New York and New England, "freed from the business and strife which he needed and enjoyed."[8]

A portion of Harriet Bill's last will and testament. *Courtesy of Bill Memorial Library.*

Harriet and Eliza Bill's family marker in the Bill Family Cemetery, Ledyard, Connecticut. *Photo by Janet Downs.*

Conveniently, when the war ended, he returned and entered into another business venture, the importing and manufacture of linen goods under the name of Tracey and Bill in New York City. Documentation indicates that company made shirts, although one reference to "bosom making" gives credence to the rumor that they manufactured ladies undergarments.[9] He bought out his partner in 1870 and sold the entire business in 1873 to retire from commercial life. He and Lucy traveled again, this time to Europe for a year; upon their return, they retired to their farm on the Thames River that Frederic had bought in 1872. (Unfortunately, it no longer exists; it became the site of a Hess Oil terminal, currently owned by Buckeye Partners. That entire waterfront area is now industrial.)

During all his years of travel and adventure, Frederic never had his sisters, Eliza and Harriet, far from his mind. In 1888, he called together a number of important men of the time and charged them with the establishment of a board of trustees for a library. Subsequent incorporation and registration with the State of Connecticut established

A bronze plaque dedicating the library to Harriet and Eliza Bill in the front hall of the library. *Photo by Janet Downs.*

Right: Portrait of Frederic Bill that hangs over the mantle in the former Trustees Rom. *Photo courtesy of Mary-Jo Shultis Photography, Bill Memorial collection.*

Below: Bill family graves, located directly behind the library. *Photo by Janet Downs.*

the Bill Memorial Library as a memorial to Frederic's sisters. The library was built in 1890 on land belonging to Frederic Bill, contiguous to the grounds of Fort Griswold Battlefield State Park. It was here that the Battle of Groton Heights had been fought during the Revolutionary War, resulting in the massacre of the American troops.

Frederic Bill, though by this time long retired, was a wealthy philanthropist committed to his community. In addition to the library, he built a sturdy brick school building next to the library to replace the former wooden structure. The Groton Heights School served as an elementary school until its closing in 2007. (Sadly, it continues to remain empty.) He also gave generously for the building of the First Congregational Church down the street.

Frederic's idyllic life as a gentleman farmer was interrupted by the death of his wife, Lucy, in April 1894. Julia Avery, who was the first (and then current) librarian of the Bill Memorial Library, wasted no time. According to local lore, she set her sights on Frederic, and he never knew what hit him. He and Julia were married in August of that same year. They immediately went abroad and visited many countries, from Norway in the north to Egypt in the south.[10] Frederic died of unknown causes in Winter Park, Florida, in 1920. Julia passed away in 1932.

Frederic, Lucy and Julia are buried directly behind the library. Frederic lies between his two wives.

STUFFED BIRDS AND LIVE BATS

The library was a stately building with a turret and leaded-glass windows, and the addition of more modern homes in the neighborhood over the years lent the library a mysterious air. For many years, ivy climbed over the stone walls and contributed to the building's somewhat foreboding appearance. Indeed, the inside was dark with soot-stained walls, mosaic tile floors and many dark corners. Only one room was available to the public at that time, as the other rooms on the first floor were the trustees' meeting room and the museum room with its collection (courtesy of Frederic's brother Gurdon) of stuffed and mounted birds, butterflies and various artifacts from all over the world, which added to the creepy atmosphere. Some of the more notable items included a stuffed walrus head, musk ox horns and a mummy's hand—part of a collection of items from the tombs of Egypt. In a *Night at the Museum* scenario, the library would have been a lively place after dark!

The stuffed birds, technically but rather morbidly referred to as "skins," were donated to a local nature center, and the rest of the collection has since been moved to a small room upstairs, where the mummy's hand has fascinated generations of locals. Often the first thing visitors will share is that they used to live in the neighborhood; then they will ask if the mummy's hand is still there. An artifact purportedly from the Valley of the Kings at Thebes, it is a small, tarry-black object with a scarab ring on the first finger. Indeed, it is still there, although for a brief time it went missing. A few preteen boys asked to visit the museum one July afternoon—not an unusual request. However, when the library was opened the next morning, there was a surprise—one of the small butterfly cases had been slipped through the mail slot. With a growing sense of panic, staff members checked the museum, and it was apparent that some of the display cases had been broken into; a few butterfly boxes and the mummy's hand were gone. When the police arrived, other children who had been in the library the previous day were able to identify the culprits. They were quickly rounded up and confessed to their deeds. They admitted that while the butterflies held little interest, they had carried the hand to an area not far from the library and proceeded to make wishes. For each wish, they broke off a finger for luck. Their luck did not last, however, as they were charged with the crime and released to the custody of their parents—all except one. When the police visited his home, it was discovered that he had left for parts unknown along with his entire family. It seems that this was not his first brush with the law!

The police were able to find all the artifacts except for one finger of the mummy's hand. When the investigation concluded, a brown paper bag containing the "remains" was returned to the library. The hand was reconstructed in its case, but it was a hasty and clumsy job. Handling the artifact was decidedly creepy, and the fingers were quickly replaced abutting the hand. The cases were then nailed shut. To this day, the missing finger is still out there—somewhere.

Although the building was thoroughly cleaned up some forty years ago and is now the gem of the neighborhood, for many children, the library is still a mysterious place. Adding to the atmosphere were bats that lived in the attic and that would sometimes get into the hollow stone walls. Their squeaks could be heard as they moved around the room inside the walls; the sound could be tracked as if they were actually in the room. Occasionally, one would make an appearance, and part of the library's inventory included what was referred to as the "bat net," an old fishing net used to capture them when they came calling. There are, in fact, probably more bat stories than ghost stories!

One of the most notorious bat encounters occurred during a Halloween story time that was conducted one morning in the library's unfinished attic, which had been decorated for the occasion with dark draperies, lanterns and other appropriate items. As the children's librarian was reading aloud, she noticed the children's heads turning this way and that. She looked up to find a bat swooping toward her. The children had been watching it fly around and were delighted; needless to say, she did not feel the same way. She quickly rounded up the children and brought them downstairs. This was the first time a bat made an active daytime appearance.

They have been found during the day, however, clinging to walls, resting in the bathroom sink and lying on the floor. On one occasion, a bat brushed the leg of a staff member when it was startled. She was also startled, and her screams reverberated through the building. Recent remediation has supposedly resolved the bat problem, but only time will tell.

THE UNEXPLAINED

While possessing an enduring interest in the paranormal, it should be noted that I, as the library director for many years, have never had premonitions, second sight or any other manifestations of sensitivity to these occurrences. I have, however, lived in a couple of places where unexplained events occurred, including apparitions, mysterious footsteps when no one was there, lights going on and alarms going off—all in the middle of the night. That being said, and given the age and public perception of the building, numerous questions have been raised over the years about whether the library was haunted. The usual answer was that, as far as anyone knew, it was not. That was the party line, and we were sticking to it.

There were, however, a number of incidents that no one could explain.

One of the first known reports came from a contractor who installed the new boiler in the basement some years ago. He reported that he put down his hammer and, the next thing he knew, it was no longer there. Assuming that one of his co-workers had moved it, he went to lunch. When he returned, the hammer was back where he had left it. But when he questioned his co-workers, he discovered that no one had been in the basement at the time the hammer disappeared. He admitted to feeling uncomfortable there and was relieved when the job was finished.

On many occasions, staff members would be unable to locate an object that had been left in one place only to discover it somewhere else later. We jokingly blamed Mr. Bill. One incident involved a typewriter that did not have a permanent location but was moved whenever anyone needed to use it. One day, in lifting it to move to it another location, we found a small sheet of paper written in faded old script that appeared to be some kind of shopping list. No one had ever seen it before; it seemed to appear out of nowhere. We were never able to explain it.

In 1994, the BML was used as a movie set for a film called *Killer: A Journal of Murder* about what was purported to be the first known serial killer in America. The rooms of the library were rearranged to accommodate the set, including a small room on the second floor that housed the library's genealogy and local history collection. The room was carefully and systematically emptied of its books and bookcases and turned into a study for President Taft, who was a character in the story. Two events stand out. On one occasion, a set designer working alone in that room heard a male voice call to him. It startled him but did not deter him from his work, although he did ask about any history of paranormal activities in the library. When the filming was over, the room was carefully put back together in its original configuration. Several days later, a paper was found on top of a bookcase in plain view. It was a document from the late 1700s conscripting a young man into military service and was signed and affixed with the original wax seal of Colonel William Ledyard, who commanded the troops at the Battle of Groton Heights in 1781. No one had ever seen this document before. While it could have fallen out of a book, it was deemed unlikely, as this room and its contents had been rearranged a number of times over the years. If previous librarians had been aware of this historically important document, it certainly would have been noted and preserved. Why was this document in the library, and how did it get there?

Then there was the smoke. For years, members of the staff would notice, independently of one another, the smell of pipe smoke. It left as quickly as it came. Everyone got used to it and teased one another that Mr. Bill was visiting. They would occasionally even talk to him and assure him that they were taking good care of his library. We would smell it, but we continued our work; it was actually somewhat comforting to think we were being watched over. We never talked about it outside the library; indeed, it wasn't discussed at all except when it occurred. Several months after my retirement, the new director asked the staff if anyone else smelled pipe smoke. She had never been told any of these stories.

Finally, in August 2014, the Thames Society of Paranormal Investigations (TSPI) was invited to conduct a formal investigation.[11] The team members set up their cameras and other equipment in various locations around the library. The monitors were in a separate location and were watched continuously by several people. The report states, "The investigation lasted about 8 hours, where paranormal events occurred in the presence of investigators and were also documented using the team's equipment."[12]

A medium—or "sensitive," as they are sometimes called—named Emma had been given no background information and was given the address of the library only an hour before the investigation. She had the impression that there were many men walking around the grounds and the neighborhood whom she believed were associated with a war. (The library property and surrounding neighborhood were open fields contiguous to the fort.) She also had a strong feeling that someone had been hanged in a nearby tree, but this could not be corroborated. Once inside the library, Emma encountered three spirits, one male and two female, who were active on the second floor and in the basement. She believed the male spirit to be that of Frederick Bill and the two females to be either his sisters or his wives.[13] The investigators picked up the sound of a woman's voice in the basement, saying, "Hello." The report notes, "In the upstairs area, she picked up on a male spirit that was tied to an object in the building. The male would never fully reveal himself to her. According to Emma, he would stand in the hallway, observing from a distance."[14] They had no idea what object it could be. The other investigator, Stephanie, also noted the strong odor of pipe smoke.

The camera in the reference room picked up the image of an orb, or circle of light, shooting across the room. Upstairs in the genealogy room, another orb can be seen clearly in the video footage entering through the door, moving across the room, landing on a bookcase and sliding down either through or behind it. The investigators also set up a flashlight that could be used to conduct "conversations" with the spirits. The switch was left in a neutral position so it could be manipulated by the spirits. At one point, Emma and Stephanie asked the spirit to turn on the light if it liked females. According to the report, "Investigator Emma asked the spirit to turn on the light if you like the females. At this time the light goes on. On the audio file you can hear some sort of an answer, and then what sounds as laughing."[15] She also asked if there were any "bad" spirits there. This time the light did not go on but a male voice can be heard saying, "No." At various times, unintelligible voices could be heard although no questions were asked. Finally, when Emma said, "Thank you," a voice responded, "You're welcome." The voices were recorded using EVP equipment.

A few weeks later the EVPs were played back by TSPI director and lead investigator Shamus Denniston. He provided no prompting; he simply played the recordings and waited for a reaction. The voices are not always easy to hear; they are muffled and covered by static. However, when distinct words or laughter came through, it was quite obvious; there was no doubt in the minds of those who were listening. In the video recordings, one can also see the light orbs crossing the room and the flashlight going on and off in response to questioning. Another segment also reveals the ghostly image of a man, seen in silhouette. A close inspection reveals a shoulder and an arm. It is hard to describe the feeling of watching and hearing these phenomena in the very building where they were recorded.

The Official Conclusion

The conclusion of the TSPI is that the property is spiritually active. As noted in the society's final report:

> *It is the opinion of TSPI that the property is "Spiritually Active," especially in the 2nd floor area Genealogy room. In the 2nd floor area, the activity is more frequent and willing to interact. It would be no surprise, if anyone spent any length of time in that area, they could witness something unusual. In this case, history has played a big part of this haunting. The activity is most likely connected to an unknown male that is present on the 2nd floor. It is possible that they are connected to the Bill Family or someone that was involved in the Battle of Groton Heights. Places that tend to have violent history can harbor spirits for* [a] *long time after they occur. Also, spirits tend to be attracted to other spirits, and may have taken up residence at the location because of its close proximity to the fort.*[16]

"The activity is most likely connected to an unknown male that is present on the 2nd floor"—the feeling is that this person is protective of the building. Those who know and love the library like to think it is Mr. Bill.

So life goes on as usual at the Bill Memorial Library. The investigation did nothing to change the daily activities of the library. The stuffed walrus head, the musk ox horns and the mummy's hand continue to share the small

The Bill Memorial Library today. *Photo by Gerry Keeler.*

museum room with the butterfly specimens on the second floor, and they remain a popular attraction. The stuffed birds are comfortably ensconced at the nature center. But in spite of the stories, the artifacts and the programs they inspire, Bill Memorial remains a modern twenty-first-century library in a beautiful antique building—with a history of unexplained activities.

But no one goes upstairs after dark.

5

The Submarine Veterans' Act II: The Play Goes On

By Hali Keeler

History

Something's afoot at the Subvets Club at 40 School Street in Groton. Mysterious noises, apparitions and unexplained movements have long been experienced in this building. But where could they have come from? This building has a long history of use by various groups. Perhaps we should start there.

The Ancient Order of United Workmen, or AOUW, was a fraternal organization begun in 1868 by John Jordan Upchurch of Meadville, Pennsylvania. Created in protest, perhaps, this organization aimed to be more responsive to the needs of workmen than were other organizations of the time. It was formed primarily to benefit workers in the "mechanical arts" or "trades," such as shipbuilding, mechanical work and carpentry, and has the distinction of being the first such organization to offer death benefit insurance to its members. Most such organizations provided for only businessmen and manufacturers.

The constitution listed the objectives as follows:

To unite into one common brotherhood all persons employed in the mechanical arts.

To create a means of prompt and effective co-operation in matters of common interest.

To oppose inimical legislation and to foster favorable legislation.

To establish libraries, provide for lectures and other means of education.
To employ all legitimate means to establish and to maintain harmony and equity between employers and employees.
To ameliorate the conditions of unfortunate, afflicted, and oppressed members.
To establish an insurance fund out of which not less than $500 should be paid to the legal heirs of a deceased member.[17]

In 1895, the Thames Lodge No. 13 of the AOUW had a building constructed at 40 School Street in Groton. It was described as a two-story building with a basement; it also included a vestibule and auditorium on the first floor. The auditorium had a good-sized stage with an entrance on each side and stairs leading to dressing rooms located below. The stage was "fitted with a pretty drop curtain and full set of scenery. A fine piano is provided for use of the orchestra."[18] It also had a gallery that served as a balcony. Why this building was constructed in such a manner is not addressed.

The building also accommodated a YMCA gymnasium on the second floor and a Lodge Room used by the Thames Lodge, the Fairview Lodge No. 101 of the International Order of Odd Fellows (IOOF) and the Independent

An old newspaper photo of the AOUW Hall after it became the Elks Lodge in 1960. *Courtesy of Jim Streeter.*

Order of Good Templars (IOGT), which was devoted to temperance and total abstinence,[19] as well as several other related groups. An image of the building can be seen on the cover of an old issue of the AOUW monthly magazine, *The Anchor and Shield*. Although it is not a clear picture it shows what the building looked like when completed in 1895.

THE THEATER

In August 1915, the AOUW hosted a movie theater in the building. According to an ad placed in the local newspaper, "Groton's New Theater in A.O.U.W. Hall," the films included *The Ingratitude of Liz Taylor: A Selig Two-Reel Comedy*, *The Sheriff's Story*, *The Fable of the Unfettered Birds* and *The Stroke of Fate*.[20] It boasted three performances daily and new pictures every day. There is no record of how long it lasted, and with three movies a day, changed daily, it would seem they would have run out of "pictures" fairly quickly! In 1939, however, an actual movie theater was built on nearby Poquonnock Road. An old poster from the Groton Theater that was found in a local consignment shop advertises, "One Night Only, November 10: *Wake of the Red Witch*, starring John Wayne and Gail Russell with a bonus 2-4-1 show, *Meet Me After the Show*, with Betty Grable and MacDonald Carey." It also advertises another John Wayne movie, a Disney film titled *The Quiet Man* to be shown December 11–13, a couple of children's matinees and, finally for December 14–16, Clifton Webb and Ginger Rogers in *Dream Boat*. Unlike the large, full-color, glossy posters typical of today's movies, all of this information is contained on a nine- by twelve-inch tan cardboard rectangle printed with red lettering. Its most recent incarnation was as a "wet paint" sign with those words scribbled in pencil on the back. The sign was rescued, but the movie theater is now a law office.

The AOUW was dissolved in 1952, and the property went into bankruptcy the following year. It passed from the estate of Ralph Smith and Milton Schwartz to public auction, where it was purchased by Charles Potkay for $2,150. Already possessing all the trappings of a theater, in the mid-1950s the building became a summer stock theater called the Groton Playhouse. An awning covered the front steps to the theater, which was entered through double doors. The box office window was directly in front, and staircases at either end of the lobby carried patrons to a gallery overlooking the main auditorium floor. Beautiful velvet opera chairs were in place for the viewers' comfort. An undated cover of a playbill was

The cover of a playbill showing a sketch of the Groton Playhouse. *Courtesy of Jim Streeter.*

found with a sketch of what the theater looked like in its heyday. It must have all been quite impressive.

On July 7, 1959, members of the Groton Rotary were introduced to the behind-the-scenes workings of a summer playhouse production. Speaking on summer stock was William Caskey, producer, and Liz Thackston, a member of the cast. Caskey said the cast were so happy to be there and had received a warm welcome from the townspeople. That prompted the playhouse to book twelve plays instead of the originally planned ten. Caskey shared his own theater background and then gave a brief rundown on the theater operations. He outlined the requirements for those who wish to become actors and the reasons for a summer stock program. Thackston also shared her theater experience and said that Groton "is a wonderful area with ideal facilities for summer stock work."[21]

The playhouse lasted for four glorious seasons from 1956 to 1959. Each week saw a new production mounted. On April 17, 1956, producer Jack Zalkind announced the summer schedule; Zalkind actually appeared in one of the August productions, although a list of that season's productions cannot be found. The plays for each season were chosen by ballots published in the local paper. The 1957 season, announced by managing director Charles Cray, opened with *Born Yesterday* on June 17, followed by such performances as *A Hatful of Rain*, *The Tender Trap*, *Arsenic and Old Lace*, *Charley's Aunt*, *Gigi* and *A Streetcar Named Desire*, to name a few. Stars of the day included actors William Feaster, Lois Markle and Naomi Riseman, who performed both in film and on Broadway. No records can be found to describe the 1958 season, but featured in the 1959 season, produced

PLAY SELECTION BALLOT

GROTON PLAYHOUSE

40 School St., Groton Tel. HI 5-4050

Born Yesterday
Charley's Aunt
Wedding Breakfast
Angel Street
Private Lives
Papa Is All
Picnic
Dracula
Anastasia
Streetcar Named Desire
Rope
The Rainmaker
Gigi
Hasty Heart
Arsenic and Old Lace
King of Hearts
Oh Men, Oh Women
Hatful of Rain
Ten Nights in a Barroom
Tender Trap
Will Success Spoil Rock Hunter
Janus

Check the 10 plays you would like to see produced at the Playhouse this summer (additional selections welcomed) and mail now to the GROTON PLAYHOUSE. The ten winning plays will be presented at the playhouse during its ten week season.

NAME ....

ADDRESS ....

A newspaper ad of the ballot of plays to be chosen by the public. *Courtesy of Jim Streeter.*

by William Caskey, was contralto Lillian Mernick, two-time winner of the Marian Anderson Award to celebrate critically acclaimed artists. In all, five concerts were given that summer.

No records are available to explain why the theater ran for only four seasons. (According to a newspaper ad in 1956, the playhouse was actively looking for rooms, apartments and houses within walking distance of the theater for the casts and crews to rent from June 30 to September 3.[22]) Was the closure due to a lack of housing, lack of money and lack of interest—or were the actors spooked by unknown activities?

In 1960, after renovations were made, the Groton Elks began using the building for their meetings until they could construct their own building on Baker's Cove in Groton. Ironically, the Elks Club in its present location was used for several years to stage dinner theater productions by local troupes. Apparently, one can take the Elks out of the theater but cannot take the theater out of the Elks!

THE RISE OF THE SUBMARINE

It should be noted that Groton is a navy town. Known as the Submarine Capital of the World, it is home to the Naval Submarine Base New London. Formerly known as the Naval Yard, it has been a fixture on the Groton side of the Thames River since 1868, when it was established as a navy yard and storage depot. It was used for the laying up of inactive ships and as a coal, then oil, refueling station for small ships. "On June 21, 1916, the Navy Yard changed forever as Commander Yeates Stirling assumed the command of the newly designated Submarine Base, the New London Submarine Flotilla, and the Submarine School. Today, Naval Submarine Base New London, our Navy's first submarine base, still proudly proclaims its motto: 'The First and Finest.'"[23]

Expanded toward the end of both world wars, the importance of the sub base was enhanced by the arrival of the first nuclear-powered submarine, the USS *Nautilus* (SSN-571) in 1954. It is now home to only fast-attack subs and is the home of the Submarine School, through which every aspiring submarine sailor must pass. The *Nautilus* has since been retired and is part of the Submarine Force Museum complex in Groton. Visitors are invited to tour the sub, as well as view the amazing displays in the adjacent building.

In 1966, the United States Submarines Veterans Inc. (USSVI), an active group of veterans who have served on submarines, raffled off a gold Cadillac in order to purchase the building at 40 School Street to use as its permanent quarters. They remain there to this day.

Since that time, the building has undergone extensive transformation. The basement, no longer housing dressing rooms, has become the Pump Room, a private club that provides food and beverages for its members. The main floor, which was occupied by the theater, is now used for events hosted by the Groton Base House Committee—meetings, luncheons, dinners and brunches. The balcony has been enclosed and houses offices, a small library and archives. The box office is barely recognizable, as it is blocked by a box fan and has been closed off. Although the stage remains, its plain utilitarian curtain (the pretty drop curtain having been replaced long ago) is closed,

The box office window today is covered with a fan window cooling unit. *Courtesy of Jim Streeter.*

and the area is adorned with flags and banners. The stage itself is used for storage. Corners and hallways are filled with boxes and other items that obscure the former grandeur of the place. The double front doors are closed off; now access is gained by ringing a bell at the basement entrance. The once beautiful building is virtually unrecognizable as a theater, although with a little imagination one can discover what lies beneath the current trappings.

THINGS GOING BUMP IN THE NIGHT

The building, particularly the Pump Room, has been rife with activities that no one can explain. Tom Connors, a longtime member who can usually be found behind the bar, is the keeper of the stories. In an interview held in June 2015, he was willing to tell a few stories about happenings over the years at 40 School Street.

First come the noises. The Saturday morning cleaning crew, working downstairs in the Pump Room, has been known to complain from time to time of noises emanating for the floor above (the former theater) when they are the only ones in the building. Are the actors still rehearsing? Moving scenery around? Rearranging the chairs? Upon investigation, there is nothing to be seen.

And what of the feelings of being touched, experienced by those clearing up after a late dinner? Tom's daughter was helping tidy up one evening after the club gave its first corned beef and cabbage dinner when she claims to have been touched though no one was there to do so. The sensation of being touched when no one is there is not an uncommon complaint; it is usually explained in the world of the paranormal as the way someone who has passed away makes his presence known.

One of the people who cooked for the club members reported that upon exiting the kitchen, she saw the swinging doors at the entrance to the Pump Room moving on their own. No one was there. It is a basement room with no windows and no chance for a strong breeze to cause movement. This phenomenon has been reported by others over the years, along with covered pool tables being mysteriously uncovered in the morning. Another phenomenon that was observed was a white mist traveling down the length of the Pump Room.

Then there was the evening when a guest left the club without properly signing out. When he returned to do so, he reported seeing a cloud moving along the shuffleboard table. When it got to the end, the cloud disappeared. Unable to explain what he saw, he left in a hurry. That would be enough to unnerve even the most seasoned sailor!

A local woman named Jennifer Emerson, a local speaker, author and museum consultant, used to go often to the club with her father, who passed away in 2007. Being sensitive and having heard the stories, she decided about ten years ago to do her own investigation. She and a friend set themselves up on the stage to see what they could find.

There are many ways to communicate with the spirit world. Methods and equipment used generally include digital EVP recorders; electromagnetic field (EMF) meters, which measure fluctuation in electromagnetic fields; and mel meters, which record changes in temperature (so named after the late daughter of the inventor). There are people who call themselves "sensitives" or "mediums" who claim to communicate directly with spirits, either by sensing or seeing; other such individuals may claim to be psychic. A flashlight with a twist on/off switch can be used to enable any entity that may be present to respond to yes or no questions.

Another method of spirit communication involves the use of a pendulum. A pendulum is simply an object tied to a string or chain that can swing freely and move in response to questions. This is what Jennifer and her friend used at the Subvets when they performed their investigation. She explained that before communicating with spirits, she envisions a circle of white protective energy around her to protect against any negative spirits and then concentrates on the goal of communicating with any spirit who might have something to say. She added:

When using a pendulum, you first make certain your body and arm are as stationary as possible to prevent a contaminated response. Then, you ask it to show you "yes" and "no." For me, usually a pendulum will swing in a clockwise circle to indicate yes, and go back and forth for no. It did so in this case, too, if memory serves me. Literally, you do it like this: "Show me yes." The pendulum moves a certain way. "Stop. Thank you. Show me no." The pendulum should move a different way this time. "Stop. Thank you."

Remember how the pendulum responded each time. Then, ask a question you already know the answer to, such as, "Is the sky blue?" Then, ask something you know is not true, such as, "Is the sun polka dot green?" If you get the correct responses for "yes" and "no," you know you've established connection with your pendulum. Then a session can begin.[24]

For this activity, Jennifer used a piece of carnelian (a red-brown semiprecious gemstone) suspended by a small chain. She and her friend then settled themselves on the stage behind the drawn curtain. They began their session by asking questions to determine what kind of yes or no questions they were able to get answers to and ended by stating that the session was ending, thanking the spirits and bidding them to go in peace. She said they also made sure to envision once again the circle of white protective light to prevent a spirit from attaching to them and perhaps accompanying them home.

Their efforts acquainted them with two spirits—Charles and Mary. Mary told them that she worked there, although in what capacity was not determined. Charles was an actor. In addition, Jennifer also reported a feeling of uneasy energy in the ladies' bathroom but was not able to determine the reason.

Research into the actors and personnel involved with the Groton Playhouse did not reveal anyone named Mary, but not all of the records have been found. Also, not all cast members were listed in the publicity found in the local papers. There was, however, a Charles Cray who was the managing director for the 1957 season who was perhaps also an actor. The new owner of the building in 1953 was also named Charles. Is it possible that he had an ulterior motive and wanted to indulge his love of performing? Several obituaries exist for individuals of that name that would fall into the approximate time period, but there is insufficient information to determine who he actually was. He may still be living, but that could not be determined either. If he has passed away, could he be the spirit with whom Jennifer communicated?

Since the building was home to a number of organizations before it was a theater, Charles and Mary may have been associated with one of these. Women were not allowed as members of the previously mentioned fraternal

The building today as the home of the Subvets. *Courtesy of Jim Streeter.*

societies at the time, but could Mary have been an office or kitchen worker? Is this her way of finally "getting in"?

We might have met with a dead end trying to ascertain the identities of Charles and Mary, but their association with the theater seems to be the most popular notion. The fact that the original building, built to be the Thames Lodge of the AOUW, was designed as a theater is puzzling. One of the organization's objectives was to "provide for lectures," but that hardly required stairway-to-basement dressing rooms, an attractive drop curtain, scenery or a piano to accompany an orchestra. The mystery seems to be part of the building itself. Or was this design common to AOUW buildings in general?

One such building in Victoria, British Columbia, staged *A Woman's Course* on March 5, 1898.[25] The AOUW in Central City, Colorado, created an addition to accommodate live theater around 1900. In 1897, the AOUW of Park City, Utah, held its first meeting in the recently built Grand Opera House, where "shows" debuted in 1898. One wonders if these buildings have resident theater ghosts as well.

Given its history and lineage, the building at 40 School Street might, in fact, be a repository of spirits in addition to Charles and Mary. Although the building bears only a slight resemblance to the original structure, those who continue to "occupy" the edifice might be happy enough that their home still stands.

6

The Rest of Us: Around the Neighborhood

By Hali Keeler and Leslie Evans

Groton Bank is a historic village on the east bank of the Thames River in Groton, Connecticut. Geographically is comprises less than a half square mile, or about 1 percent of the town of Groton. In 1655, the ferry operator Cary Latham became the first permanent English settler on the east bank of the Thames when it was part of the Pequot Colony, later to become New London. After Groton became a separate town in 1705, the east bank of the river became known as Groton Bank and grew to become a major village in the town.

In the following centuries, Fort Griswold, located in Groton Bank, was the site of the only major Revolutionary War battle in Connecticut (September 6, 1781) and was a key defense for the Thames Harbor and Connecticut in the War of 1812. Groton Bank became a national and world leader in shipbuilding; an active participant in the West Indies trade; a transportation hub and the town's early center of business and commerce. It was home to the most famous captains of the whaling era as well as other prominent sea captains and was the residence of many leading citizens, including a congressman.[26]

The main street of the area, originally called Bank Road, was eventually changed to Thames Street. In an article from the local newspaper in 1913, Elizabeth Avery describes this street in the village of Groton Bank. In her words, Thames Street is

The site of New London Ferry Landing, formerly that of Cary Latham. *Courtesy of the Avery-Copp Museum–Jim Streeter Collection.*

> *this winding path along the riverbank* [that] *has been the main thoroughfare and for many years the only one of Groton Bank. The word Bank was added to the name of the village on account of its location and to distinguish it from Center Groton, which was at one period an equally important portion of the town. This street formerly called Bank Road now bearing the name of the English river, naturally would have also the pronunciation of the old home stream "Tems" pleasant and dear to the ears of Winthrop and his colonists; "Thames, or Tamez," being a localism that has gradually come somewhat into use but would have been quite unfamiliar to the early settlers.*[27]

A bustling center of commerce until the late 1950s, Thames Street was once home to a variety of businesses, including Carlos Allyn's grocery, Edgecomb and Poppe dry goods, Coe & Bailey general store, Decarolis Shoe Repair, Macy's Barber Shop, Krieger's drugstore and the Groton Hotel. A number of public buildings, including a large brick post office, Groton Utilities, the city police station and a state police barracks made Thames Street a true "downtown." The Groton Bank Historic District was listed on the National Register of Historic Places in 1983. Today, it is a shadow of its former self, but there are still a number of businesses, including a restaurant, a tackle shop, a barber and several legal offices, that continue to operate there. A recent reconstruction of the street and sidewalks, along with planned improvements to the streetscape, give residents the hope that one day the street will resume its former importance in Groton Bank.

At the corner of Thames and Latham Streets is a stone marker memorializing the former site of the Ebenezer Avery House. Built by Parke Avery in the 1750s as a home for his third son, Ebenezer, the house was situated not far from the ferry landing. Lieutenant Ebenezer Avery (not to be confused with Ensign Ebenezer Avery or Captain Ebenezer Avery) fought and was injured in the Battle of Groton Heights. His house was used as a hospital for the wounded and dying after the battle. Those soldiers who fell in the vicinity of the fort were loaded into a large wagon by the British with the thought of bringing them down to the river so they could be taken away as prisoners on the waiting ships. The wagon proved too heavy and got away from the men in charge of it, rolling at high speed downhill until it crashed into an apple tree near the river bank. The wagon exploded on impact, throwing the wounded in all directions. The dead and dying were brought into the nearby Ebenezer Avery house to be cared for.

Ebenezer Avery House (lower left corner) in its original location, looking up the hill. *Courtesy of the Avery-Copp Museum–Jim Streeter Collection.*

The granite marker at the original site of the Ebenezer Avery House, at the corner of Thames and Latham Streets. *Photo courtesy of Janet Downs.*

The Millstone memorial to those who were carried off in British ships after the massacre. *Photo courtesy of Janet Downs.*

It is said that their screams could be heard clearly across the river in New London and were reportedly heard on many nights for years afterward. Across the street from this site, where the apple tree once stood, rests a large millstone inscribed and dedicated to the memory of those who perished.

THE HOUSE IN THE FORT

For many years after the battle, the house remained in the Avery family. Descendants did not wash away the bloodstains on the floor that were left from the battle; they remained as a memorial to the defenders and were visible for well over a century before they were eventually obliterated by normal wear and tear.

The Ebenezer Avery House was moved to a site in the lower part of Fort Griswold just prior to the bicentennial in 1976. The house had fallen into disrepair, and the ground floor had been used as a shop with an apartment above; it was slated to be torn down in order to build apartments. G. Stanton Avery, a descendant, paid to have it dismantled, moved, reassembled board by board and restored so that it would be preserved.

Ebenezer Avery House. *Courtesy of the Avery-Copp Museum–Jim Streeter Collection.*

Ebenezer Avery House parlor. *Courtesy of the Avery-Copp Museum–Jim Streeter Collection.*

Ebenezer Avery House dining room. *Courtesy of the Avery-Copp Museum–Jim Streeter Collection.*

Ebenezer Avery House bedroom. *Courtesy of the Avery-Copp Museum–Jim Streeter Collection.*

Ebenezer Avery House today. *Photo courtesy of Janet Downs.*

The house is now owned and maintained by the Avery Family Association, incorporated in 1895 as a nonprofit. The association is responsible for the care and upkeep of the house (in conjunction with the State of Connecticut, on whose land it sits) and several other important Avery sites in Groton.

Modern ghost stories include experiences reported by Groton Utilities employees when they have entered the basement to read the electric meter. Footsteps have been clearly heard upstairs walking around the house. The first time it was thought that a museum employee had arrived for work, but no one was there when the utility worker came upstairs. This has happened several times; now two people go in together when it is time to check the meter.

ACTIVITY ON THAMES STREET

Along Thames Street there are several commercial buildings that tell tales. What was formerly a post office is now the home of the Fleet Reserve Association Branch 20, a nonprofit veterans' organization begun in 1924 that represents the interests of enlisted members of the "Sea Service"—the navy, marines and Coast Guard.[28] At some point in the 1930s, this building also housed the medical infirmary of Dr. Tyson Hughes.

One night in 2011, a new bartender began working there. She described closing up for the evening before realizing that she had left something inside. She debated not going back in but decided it was too important, so she went in. Immediately upon entering, she heard a man whistling. The hair stood up on the back of her neck, but by the time she had retrieved her item, the whistling had stopped. As she was leaving, she made a decision that if they were both going to spend time there, they should become friends. She told the "ghost" that it was OK and that he could continue his song. As she locked up for the second time, the whistling began again.

The woman still works there in spite of what she experienced; she said she often feels a male presence and is comfortable with it. Thanks to modern technology, she has been able to document some of her experiences. She has downloaded a "ghost detector app" to her phone. It uses sensors to detect sources of variable magnetic emissions which could indicate paranormal activity. Using EVPs (electronic voice phenomena), it picks up transmissions, which it then translates into words. Sitting near it during an interview, one could hear random words emanating from the device. Words included *shame*, *envy*, *vast*, *evil*, *male*, *bright* and *annoyed*, among many others. The camera also takes unprompted photos when energy is detected. Previous photos have revealed orbs of light; one photo depicted a swirl of light on an otherwise plain dark tabletop where we sat.

Possibly the most convincing pieces of evidence that the Fleet Reserve building is host to otherworldly guests are two photographs. The first is of a couple who had their picture taken standing in front of the building in July 2009. When the photo was given to them later, there was a shadowy figure between them. The other photograph is of several women enjoying a party. Although they saw and heard nothing, over the shoulder of one is the ghostly white image of a face, which looks like it is whispering into her ear.

Almost directly across the street from the Fleet Reserve is an empty storefront that was originally a hotel and at various times since then an army surplus store, an appliance store and a YMCA. When it was the army surplus store, there was an intercom connecting the first floor and the basement. According to a gentleman who spent quite a bit of time in this shop, occasionally the intercom would transmit the sounds of children playing from the empty basement.

Farther south on Thames Street is a building that was formerly Macy's Barber Shop, shuttered for many years. It was given new life several years ago as Danielle's Barber Shop, and the owner chose to retain the original fixtures, including the barber chairs and photos on the wall. Although thoroughly modernized where it was needed, it still has the air of an old-fashioned tonsorial parlor. A rotating barber pole has also been affixed to the outside of the shop. (Incidentally, in times long past barbers also pulled teeth and performed surgery. The red stripes represented bloody bandages wrapped around a pole, signifying the locations of such a business!) The barbers who work in this shop tell many stories of occurrences they cannot explain, such as opening the shop after the weekend to find the radio on, electric clippers that don't work and instruments found in places other than where they were left. The radio occasionally goes on and off during business hours as well.

Andrew Scibelli succeeded his father as the barber there when it was Macy's, and he passed away in 1999. He left behind traces of his tenure, such as bowling score cards tucked into the corners of drawers. The current barbers leave them there as a reminder. Could the figure standing in the doorway that one of the barbers sometimes catches from the corner of her eye be "Andy"? Another barber describes the occasional sudden feeling of cool air, as if someone was walking past.

Danielle's barbershop, former site of Macy's Barber Shop. *Photo courtesy of Gerry Keeler.*

While Andy is truly a silent partner, he remains an accepted member of the staff. He is frequently spoken to, kindly, so he can still feel at home.

LATHAM STREET

Nearby on Latham Street are a number of houses that have had their share of mysterious happenings over the years. One was the home of a successful whaling captain until his ship disappeared on an Arctic voyage in 1883. His widow and his brother, who was also a sea captain, held out hope for years that he was still alive and would soon be coming home. His widow eventually moved out of the house and built a new one nearby, just around the corner. During the past century, the original house became a rental property but had great difficulty keeping tenants because people claimed the house was haunted and would quickly move out. Complaints centered on doors slamming, windows opening and closing and, especially troubling, a "presence" that would push from behind when someone was descending the stairs. It was described as not so much a physical push as a definite "force." About twenty or so years ago, the house was purchased by the current owner and returned to a single-family dwelling. She also had the experience of feeling that she was being "pushed" from behind. Finally, after a particularly harrowing episode when she felt she was indeed being pushed down the stairs, this forceful lady confronted the ghost and insisted that she wasn't leaving so they would have to find a way to live together. Did the captain lost at sea

A house on Latham Street with paranormal activity. *Photo courtesy of Janet Downs.*

finally return, and was he bothered that his wife didn't wait for him? The current resident has not been troubled since.

A neighboring house, built in 1870, harbors a ghostly presence that makes itself known not by sounds or disruptive activities but by smells. Occasionally and unpredictably, when coming upstairs from the cellar into the kitchen, the residents are confronted by the smells of cooking when none is actually taking place. Most common is the smell of bread baking. Also occurring frequently are the smell of beef stew and the distinctive odor of cooked cabbage.

In yet another house on Latham Street, a man who lived in an apartment from 2010 to 2013 reported that his cat would sit very still, staring fixedly at nothing that was apparent to him while meowing plaintively. Although legend has it that cats are often the "familiars" of witches, he never knew what—or whom—the cat saw.

Baker Avenue abuts the south side of Fort Griswold, previously mentioned in conjunction with unexplained activities. A local resident was around twelve years old when he lived in a house there. One evening, he was helping his father close up the family business on Thames Street when his mother called him to come home. She and his sister were hearing strange noises in the attic and wanted him to investigate. When he entered the attic, a metal helmet flew across the room at him and landed on the floor. Subsequently, he and his sister would experiment by positioning papers on a table in that same area of the attic, only to find them on the floor the next day. The helmet had belonged to his brother, who was a lifeguard at the time when that kind of hat was popular. They don't know who threw it, but something in that attic had a very good aim.

SEA CAPTAINS

On nearby Monument Street, many of the houses were built by prosperous sea captains during the nineteenth century. Some made their fortunes in maritime trade, some from whaling; these houses were meant to be tangible expressions of their wealth. Not all mariners survived to enjoy a comfortable old age. Their ventures had the potential for great rewards but only because they took great risks, braving winter storms and tropical hurricanes, attacks by pirates and enemy war ships, injury aboard ship, exposure to tropical diseases and hostile natives in many parts of the world. If someone died aboard ship, he would be hastily buried at sea. Instead of a coffin, a shroud would be made of sail canvas and sewn up around the deceased. A superstition held that the last stitch should pass through the nose so that, if by some chance the person was still alive, the pain would cause him to react. A burial service would be conducted by the captain, and the body would be slid overboard to slip beneath the waves. Cemeteries throughout coastal New England have stones memorializing men who died at sea.

An exception to the sea burial described above was the fairly uncommon practice of preserving a body to bring it home for burial. This method would be used only if the deceased were a captain or a very important passenger and generally only if the person died on the homeward leg of the voyage. The deceased was put into a barrel of alcohol—rum, Madeira wine or whatever was available. This would delay decomposition long enough to bring the body home for burial.

One of the prominent sea captains of the time was Captain Ebenezer "Rattler" Morgan and his house, located on Monument Street, still stands. He was quite successful, as this narrative explains:

> *Ebenezer Morgan, better known as "Rattler" Morgan…made the best whaling voyage on record; sailing June 4, 1864, for Hudson's Bay,* [the

The home of Captain Ebenezer "Rattler" Morgan, who planted the first American flag on Alaskan soil. *Courtesy of the Avery-Copp Museum–Jim Streeter Collection.*

> ship] *returned September 18, 1865, with 1,391 barrels of whale oil, and 22,650 pounds of whalebone, a cargo worth $150,000, while the outlay for vessel and fitting was but $35,800. This was the best whaling voyage ever made. The principle on which whaling was conducted was co-operative, the owners furnishing ship, outfit, and providing for the honoring of the captain's drafts; the captain was quite often a part or whole owner. Capital had two-thirds of the gain and the other third was divided proportionately among the officers and men. There being no wages settled, every incentive was furnished for diligence, and sometimes a bonus was offered to the first man who sighted a whale.*[29]

Morgan was also the first man to plant an American flag in Alaskan territory after its cession to the United States from Russia.

Another whaler who lived on the same street was Captain James Monroe Buddington. His ship rescued the ship HMS *Resolute*, which was trapped in ice and abandoned. Although the ship was returned to Queen Victoria in 1856, its timbers where used to build the desk that Queen Victoria gifted to President Rutherford B. Hayes. It has been used by U.S. presidents ever since.

THE SURROUNDING AREA

On Meridian Street is a small red house, built in 1717, that was one of the few structures standing in this area at the time of the revolution. Most of the buildings in this neighborhood were located along the river at that time, and the land surrounding the house was an open field cleared for agriculture. The house was owned by Patrick Ward, one of the defenders killed at Fort Griswold. In the early twentieth century, when sewer pipes were being installed on this street, the excavation uncovered human remains. Artifacts like buttons and buckles indicated that the remains belonged to British soldiers killed at Fort Griswold. At least fifty British soldiers were buried on or near the battlefield. Between the time of the battle and the installation of sewer lines, streets were laid out on these fields, and quite a few houses were built over what were certainly the resting places of British soldiers.

Between the library and the Patrick Ward house is one such residence. Although not built until the 1940s, it stands on land that would have been open at the time of the battle. The current owners have reported hearing, on several occasions, the sound of a group of men marching, with equipment rattling as they walk. The first time, they thought it was a group of reenactors in the street, but no one was there when they looked out. Usually, the sounds start outside and then seem to come through the basement. Militia certainly would have marched through this area as they answered the call to defend the fort. The owners became perturbed enough to eventually bring in someone whom they felt could rid the house of these unwelcomed guests. The residents have been appeased, but no one can say the same for those who marched. Perhaps they are marching still.

Another home dating from the 1800s and located on nearby Cottage Street has been reputed to have "company." A former owner reported that while he was stripping old wallpaper, he experienced continual interference from an unseen force that would hide his tools. While another resident who had grown up in the home never experienced any such activities, she did report that it was her mother who had put up the wallpaper. Brought to the house as a bride, she was then expected to care for her ailing mother-in-law. She was unhappy to be living in this house and grew very disagreeable in her old age. Perhaps the presence is her mother protesting the change. The wallpaper may have been the only thing that brought her pleasure during her tenure there.

SPICER AVENUE

In 1879, a majestic Victorian house was built on nearby Church Street on a large tract of land. Owned by Helen M. Allen, it bears a slight resemblance to the Addams family mansion from 1960s television. In the late 1890s, the land was subdivided and a street was created on the south side of the house. (Called Allen Street at the time, it was later renamed Spicer Avenue.) In 1900, on the parcel directly behind the Allen house, legend has it that the duplex house built there was for the two daughters of the owner; later construction of a driveway uncovered electrical and water lines running from the Victorian to the duplex. A search of records does not give us their names although we may assume they were Allens. The property changed hands several times over the years, and by 1965, it was owned and inhabited by well-known local realtor Lian Obrey. She reports that their very first Thanksgiving in that house was memorable for more than the obvious reason. At one point during the meal, as the family was seated around the dining room table, they heard a noise at the heavy front door. Their first thought was that one of the dogs had jumped on it, but in fact, the door had opened. The family members then, in turn, felt a chill go past each person around the table. When the children expressed alarm, Lian simply told them to pull up another chair. The chill settled in that spot. This presence apparently enjoyed the holidays, as the chill would arrive at each celebration.

So who was this person? The family was adept at using a Ouija board and discovered in their sessions that their "ghost" was a friendly woman who felt it was her job to watch over the children. After this revelation, one of the children, who had never been able to sleep with her door closed, did so from then on, feeling safe and protected.

Another of the children who had since moved out came back to live there when he was newly married. He reported that on several nights, he would awaken to see the image of a woman in white standing by the bed. She just stood there for a while and then left. This young man's wife never saw her but knew when she was there because she would be awakened by her husband, shaking with fright.

As a realtor, Lian had the opportunity to visit many houses where she felt a definite presence—mostly good ones (although she had encountered some where she simply would not enter). Among her many paranormal experiences, one stands out. It was an old inn, and as she came down the back stairs, she saw a little boy in the kitchen. She thought she was alone in the building and saw no other cars outside. She questioned him about the whereabouts of his parents, and his responses were shakes or nods of his head. Of course when she left the room to investigate, he disappeared. If she says a house has a presence, I am inclined to believe her.

Coincidentally, a house just several doors up also has a story to tell. The former owner tells of a kindly woman wearing a pink floral dress and a hat. They could often smell her, a pleasant scent unlike any that the homeowners wore. Although the house was built during the Edwardian era (1909), the woman's clothing seemed more Victorian in style. At some point in the past, the master bedroom had been remodeled; she appeared there fairly regularly, coming in through the wall where the door used to be. Often she just disappeared, but on occasion, she went across the room and left through an unused side door. The owner would be in bed and watch her come and go. She appeared in that bedroom only, save for two times when she was seen in the dining room, coming in though the archway from the formal living room.

AND FINALLY

Although most of the houses mentioned were built by descendants of the English colonists, the domestic servants and manual laborers in this neighborhood were mostly Irish, Scottish and Italian. Each of these cultural groups had its own folklore and superstitions.

Halloween was not a holiday that was observed by New Englanders until after the middle of the nineteenth century, but it was well established in Ireland, Scotland and Wales, having evolved from ancient Celtic beliefs. Immigrants brought the tradition to America with them. By 1900, Halloween had become a secular holiday, with a child-centered community focus. Jack-o'-lanterns were long a Halloween tradition, but in Ireland, they were made from turnips. Pumpkins were adopted once they became available, as they are much larger and easier to carve. Modern decorations on house fronts did not make their appearance in this area until after World War II.

An important element of Irish folklore is the banshee, which is a Gaelic word for "fairy woman." The banshee is an attendant fairy that follows the old Irish families and wails before a death. Many have reported seeing her, usually in the form of an old woman with long, silvery hair. She moves by gliding rather than walking and often has a mist about her. She does not speak or interact with anyone, nor does she cause harm. Nevertheless, she strikes terror into the hearts of those who encounter her. Sometimes, she is not seen at all, but her moaning, shrieking, wailing cry of grief and despair is unmistakable. The question of whom she was crying for would usually be answered later when it was discovered that someone had died during the night or been killed in an accident the next day.

One or two hundred years ago, this neighborhood would have looked very different. It would have been darker, as there were no street lights. (Electricity was not in use in this area until around 1907, and the Avery-Copp House was one of the first to get it.) Soft light would glow from inside houses from the gas lamps used at the time. It would have been quieter, as there was none of the traffic noise that is a persistent backdrop today. Automobiles were not introduced until about 1900, but there would have been people on foot, in carriages and on horseback at least until the 1920s. Even the smells were different—burning leaves, coal and wood smoke from stoves used for heating and cooking and those scents associated with horses and other animals.

If you open your mind and your senses, perhaps you can imagine the spirits that roam here, claiming the Groton Bank neighborhood as their own. They might be soldiers, sea captains, servants or ordinary residents from long ago. On still, dark nights, their presence can still be felt among us.

NOTES

1. Kimball, *Groton Story*, 38–41.
2. Harris, *Battle of Groton Heights*, 47–52.
3. Ibid., 53–55.
4. Pitkin, *New England Ghosts*, 96.
5. *Genealogical and Biographical Record*, 168.
6. Ibid.
7. Bill; *History of the Bill Family*, 305–6
8. Ibid.
9. "Some Old New York," 41.
10. *Genealogical and Biographical Record*, 168.
11. Thames Society for Paranormal Investigation, interview by the author.
12. Denniston, "TSPI Case Report," 3.
13. Ibid.
14. Ibid.
15. Ibid.
16. Ibid.
17. Equilibri-Yum, "Ancient Order of United Workmen."
18. Ibid.
19. "FAQs," IOGT International.
20. "Groton's New Theater," *New London Day*, August 24, 1915, 8.
21. "Two from Playhouse Address Rotary," *New London Day*, July 8, 1959, 7.
22. "Wanted!" *New London Day*, May 23, 1956, 18.
23. U.S. Navy, "CNIC Naval Submarine Base New London."

24. Jennifer M. Emerson, interview by the author.
25. Evans, *Frontier Theater*, 165.
26. Althuis, "Groton Bank–History."
27. Avery, "Development and History of Ancient Streets of Groton."
28. "About FRA," Fleet Reserve Association.
29. Marshall, *Modern History*, 79.

BIBLIOGRAPHY

"About FRA." Fleet Reserve Association. http://www.fra.org/fra/web.

Althuis, Thomas. "Groton Bank–History." Groton Bank Historical Association. http://www.grotonbankha.com.

Avery, Elizabeth M. "Development and History of Ancient Streets of Groton." *New London Day*, April 12, 1913.

Bill, Ledyard, ed. *History of the Bill Family*. N.p., 1867.

Connors, Tom. Interview by the author. Subvets Club, Groton, CT. June 18, 2015.

Denniston, Shamus. Interview by the author. Groton, CT. October 2014.

———. "TSPI Case Report." In Thames Society of Paranormal Investigations (TSPI) Case Report. N.p., 2014. 1–4.

Emerson, Jennifer M. Interview by the author. Groton, CT. October 26, 2015.

Equilibri-Yum. "Ancient Order of United Workmen." The Infomercantile. http://www.infomercantile.com/-/Ancient_Order_Of_United_Workmen.

Evans, Chad. *Frontier Theater: A History of Nineteenth Century Theatrical Entertainment in the Canadian Far West and Alaska*. Victoria, BC: Sono Nis Press, 1983.

"FAQs." IOGT International. http://iogt.org.

F.M.C. "Memoir of Anna Bailey of Groton." *New London Weekly Chronicle*, January 21, 1851.

Genealogical and Biographical Record of New London County, Connecticut: Containing Biographical Sketches of Prominent and Representative Citizens and Genealogical

Records of Many of the Early Settled Families. New London, CT: J.H. Beers and Company, 1905.

Harris, William Wallace. *The Battle of Groton Heights: A Collection of Narratives, Official Reports, Records, Etc., of the Storming of Fort Griswold, the Massacre of Its Garrison, and the Burning of New London by British Troops*. New London, CT: C. Allyn, 1882.

Kimball, Carol W. *The Groton Story*. Rev. ed. Groton, CT: Groton Public Library, 1991.

———. *Remembering Groton: Tales from East of the Thames*. Charleston, SC: The History Press, 2008.

Lorenz, Carl. "Mother Bailey, Inscribed in Her Memory." Song for the 100th anniversary of Mother Bailey's birth. Boston: Oliver Diston Company, 1858.

Marshall, Benjamin Tinkham. *A Modern History of New London County, Connecticut*. New London, CT: Lewis Historical Publishing Company, 1922.

New London Day. "Groton's New Theater." August 24, 1915, 9–8.

———. "Wanted!" May 23, 1956, 18.

Pitkin, David. *New England Ghosts*. Chestertown, NY: Aurora Publications, 2010.

"Some Old New York City Shirt Manufacturers." *Clothier and Furnisher* 46 (August 1, 1872): 42.

Stark, Charles R. *Groton CT 1705–1905*. Stonington, CT: Palmer Press, 1922.

Thames Society for Paranormal Investigation. Interview by the author. Groton, CT. October 2014.

U.S. Navy. "CNIC Naval Submarine Base New London." CNIC Naval Submarine Base New London. http://www.cnic.navy.mil/regions/cnrma/installations/navsubbase_new_london/about/history.html.

About the Author

Hali Keeler retired in 2014 as the director of the Bill Memorial Library, one of the sites featured in the book, in Groton. Even after thirty-five years there, she was surprised to find out the place was "spiritually active"—although that may account for some odd events over the years. She is passionate about local history and belongs to several groups and associations in Groton Bank, where she also makes her home. She also served on city committees concerning the renovation of Thames Street and the updated Plan for Conservation and Development of the area. Her house was built in 1880 and is not haunted.

A Connecticut native, she is also an adjunct professor at Three Rivers Community College in Norwich in its Library Technical Assistant program and has written two textbooks for library support staff. She has a BS, MA and MLS. She wrote the chapters "The Bill Memorial Library: No Smoking, Please!"; "The Submarine Veterans' Act II: The Play Goes On"; and "The Rest of Us: Around the Neighborhood," with Leslie Evans.

About the Contributors

Leslie Evans is the director of the Avery-Copp House, a historic house museum interpreting local history on Thames Street in Groton, Connecticut. An independent historian whose interests focus on domestic life, she enjoys teaching about the experiences of the people who lived and worked in Groton during centuries past. Born and raised in Canada, she came to Groton via California and is a resident of Groton Bank, living in a house built in 1870. She is a member of the Friends of Fort Griswold, the Groton Bank Historical Association and the Groton Historic Society and is an advocate for the preservation of historic buildings in the neighborhood, including the Anna Warner Bailey House.

Leslie holds a BA and MA from Smith College. She hopes this book will encourage others to explore the rich history of the region, haunted or not. She is the author of the chapters "The Mother Bailey House: Anna Warner Bailey," "The Avery-Copp House: If These Walls Could Talk" and, with Hali Keeler, "The Rest of Us: Around the Neighborhood."

David Rose retired in 2015 as registrar of voters in Groton and retired from Pfizer Inc. in 2004 after forty-one years. He has a passion for local history, sparked when, at the age of twelve, he moved to Groton Borough in a house just down the hill from Fort Griswold. He belongs to several historic groups and associations in Historic Groton Bank, where he also makes his home. He is a charter member and past president of the Friends of Fort Griswold and a member of the Groton Bank Historical Association.

A Connecticut native and lifelong resident, David is an unofficial docent of Fort Griswold Battlefield State Park who takes every opportunity he can to explain to visitors what occurred at the fort and the impact the battle had on the community. He has a BS in education from Southern Illinois University and an MS in management from Rensselaer Polytechnic Institute. David is responsible for the chapter "Fort Griswold: Still on Watch?"

CPSIA information can be obtained
at www.ICGtesting.com
Printed in the USA
LVHW031923030220
645690LV00013B/799